Problems of Death

O P P O S I N G   V I E W P O I N T S ®

Other Books of Related Interest

Problems of Death
OPPOSING VIEWPOINTS ®

James D. Torr and Laura K. Egendorf, *Book Editors*

David L. Bender, *Publisher*
Bruno Leone, *Executive Editor*
Bonnie Szumski, *Editorial Director*
David M. Haugen, *Managing Editor*

OPPOSING
VIEWPOINTS®
SERIES

Greenhaven Press, Inc., San Diego, California

Library of Congress Cataloging-in-Publication Data

Problems of death : opposing viewpoints / James D. Torr, book
    editor, Laura K. Egendorf, book editor
        p.   cm. — (Opposing viewpoints series)
    Includes bibliographical references and index.
    ISBN 0-7377-0350-4 (lib. bdg. : alk. paper) —
    ISBN 0-7377-0349-0 (pbk. : alk. paper)

Greenhaven Press, Inc., P.O. Box 289009
San Diego, CA 92198-9009

"Congress shall make no law...abridging the freedom of speech, or of the press."

First Amendment to the U.S. Constitution

The basic foundation of our democracy is the First Amendment guarantee of freedom of expression. The Opposing Viewpoints Series is dedicated to the concept of this basic freedom and the idea that it is more important to practice it than to enshrine it.

Contents

Why Consider Opposing Viewpoints?

"The only way in which a human being can make some approach to knowing the whole of a subject is by hearing what can be said about it by persons of every variety of opinion and studying all modes in which it can be looked at by every character of mind. No wise man ever acquired his wisdom in any mode but this."

John Stuart Mill

In our media-intensive culture it is not difficult to find differing opinions. Thousands of newspapers and magazines and dozens of radio and television talk shows resound with differing points of view. The difficulty lies in deciding which opinion to agree with and which "experts" seem the most credible. The more inundated we become with differing opinions and claims, the more essential it is to hone critical reading and thinking skills to evaluate these ideas. Opposing Viewpoints books address this problem directly by presenting stimulating debates that can be used to enhance and teach these skills. The varied opinions contained in each book examine many different aspects of a single issue. While examining these conveniently edited opposing views, readers can develop critical thinking skills such as the ability to compare and contrast authors' credibility, facts, argumentation styles, use of persuasive techniques, and other stylistic tools. In short, the Opposing Viewpoints Series is an ideal way to attain the higher-level thinking and reading skills so essential in a culture of diverse and contradictory opinions.

In addition to providing a tool for critical thinking, Opposing Viewpoints books challenge readers to question their own strongly held opinions and assumptions. Most people form their opinions on the basis of upbringing, peer pressure, and personal, cultural, or professional bias. By reading carefully balanced opposing views, readers must directly confront new ideas as well as the opinions of those with whom they disagree. This is not to simplistically argue that everyone who reads opposing views will—or should—change his or her opinion. Instead, the series enhances readers' understanding of their own views by encouraging confrontation with opposing ideas. Careful examination of others' views can lead to the readers' understanding of the logical inconsistencies in their own opinions, perspective on why they hold an opinion, and the consideration of the possibility that their opinion requires further evaluation.

Evaluating Other Opinions

To ensure that this type of examination occurs, Opposing Viewpoints books present all types of opinions. Prominent spokespeople on different sides of each issue as well as well-known professionals from many disciplines challenge the reader. An additional goal of the series is to provide a forum for other, less known, or even unpopular viewpoints. The opinion of an ordinary person who has had to make the decision to cut off life support from a terminally ill relative, for example, may be just as valuable and provide just as much insight as a medical ethicist's professional opinion. The editors have two additional purposes in including these less known views. One, the editors encourage readers to respect others' opinions—even when not enhanced by professional credibility. It is only by reading or listening to and objectively evaluating others' ideas that one can determine whether they are worthy of consideration. Two, the inclusion of such viewpoints encourages the important critical thinking skill of objectively evaluating an author's credentials and bias. This evaluation will illuminate an author's reasons for taking a particular stance on an issue and will aid in readers' evaluation of the author's ideas.

As series editors of the Opposing Viewpoints Series, it is our hope that these books will give readers a deeper understanding of the issues debated and an appreciation of the complexity of even seemingly simple issues when good and honest people disagree. This awareness is particularly important in a democratic society such as ours in which people enter into public debate to determine the common good.

Those with whom one disagrees should not be regarded as enemies but rather as people whose views deserve careful examination and may shed light on one's own.

Thomas Jefferson once said that "difference of opinion leads to inquiry, and inquiry to truth." Jefferson, a broadly educated man, argued that "if a nation expects to be ignorant and free . . . it expects what never was and never will be." As individuals and as a nation, it is imperative that we consider the opinions of others and examine them with skill and discernment. The Opposing Viewpoints Series is intended to help readers achieve this goal.

David L. Bender & Bruno Leone,
Series Editors

———————————

Greenhaven Press anthologies primarily consist of previously published material taken from a variety of sources, including periodicals, books, scholarly journals, newspapers, government documents, and position papers from private and public organizations. These original sources are often edited for length and to ensure their accessibility for a young adult audience. The anthology editors also change the original titles of these works in order to clearly present the main thesis of each viewpoint and to explicitly indicate the opinion presented in the viewpoint. These alterations are made in consideration of both the reading and comprehension levels of a young adult audience. Every effort is made to ensure that Greenhaven Press accurately reflects the original intent of the authors included in this anthology.

———————————

Introduction

"Neither the sun nor death can be looked at with a steady eye."

—*Francis, duc de La Rochefoucauld, Maxim 26*

Each year, over 32,000 people commit suicide in the United States. In Oregon in 1997, 15 terminally ill patients took advantage of a newly enacted law legalizing physician-assisted suicide and committed suicide with doctor-prescribed lethal medication. Approximately 1.37 million abortions were performed in the United States in 1996. Finally, 74 prisoners were executed in the United States in 1997, while 3,335 more remained on death row.

Is there a relationship among these statistics? Many people believe there is. They contend that increased acceptance of abortion, physician-assisted suicide, and the death penalty are hallmarks of a "culture of death" that grips modern society. The following quote—excerpted from a speech given by Allan Carlson, president of the Howard Center for Family, Religion, and Society, at a meeting of pro-life leaders on January 9, 1998—typifies this point of view:

> We gather to mark the 25th anniversary of the *Roe v. Wade* decision by the United States Supreme Court, handed down by the justices on January 22, 1973. This decision voided laws banning or regulating abortion in all fifty states and made abortion a "free choice.". . . Looking back from our present time, we can see this decision as part of a first step in inaugurating a Culture of Death in this country, one where the abortion of over one million unborn babies annually would soon be joined by assisted suicide, "partial birth" infanticide, and other cowardly modern answers to age-old human problems.

In the view of pro-lifers such as Carlson, abortion, assisted suicide (sometimes referred to as euthanasia), and capital punishment are all forms of killing and thus morally problematic. This view was recently expounded by Pope John Paul II in his March 25, 1995, encyclical letter, *Evangelium Vitae*, or "The Gospel of Life," in which he warns of "an extremely dangerous crisis of the moral sense, which is

13

becoming more and more incapable of distinguishing between good and evil, even when the fundamental right to life is at stake."

"The direct and voluntary killing of an innocent human being is always gravely immoral," states the pope. In "The Gospel of Life" he reiterates the Catholic Church's adamant opposition to abortion as an "unspeakable crime," to suicide as a "gravely evil choice," and to euthanasia as "a disturbing 'perversion' of true mercy." Furthermore, John Paul II argues that the death penalty is only justified when society has no other means of protecting itself from dangerous criminals, and that "today, . . . as a result of steady improvements in the organization of the penal system, such cases are very rare, if not practically non-existent." Moreover, warns the pope, the growing acceptance of abortion, euthanasia, and the death penalty are part of an alarming trend in modern society: "We are facing an enormous and dramatic clash between good and evil, death and life, the 'culture of death' and the 'culture of life.'"

Of course, "The Gospel of Life" was immediately criticized by pro-choice groups, right-to-die activists, and many death penalty supporters. In particular, many pro-choice groups do not view abortion as a "problem of death" at all, and so found the pope's identification of abortion as murder preposterous. Trish Hooper, writing in the *New York Times*, states, "The value of life is never more fully confirmed than when a woman decides not to continue with a pregnancy that would result in yet another unwanted life." She dismisses "The Gospel of Life" as out of touch with the lives of modern Catholics and Americans in general: "Many of them may find it more Christian to follow their consciences when it comes to abortion than to follow the commands of this pope."

Similarly, although the pope and many pro-life organizations group abortion, assisted suicide, and the death penalty together as part of a culture of death, individuals who support these issues often do not see them that way at all. Pro-choice individuals are concerned with a woman's right to control her own body; death penalty supporters are concerned with criminal justice; and supporters of assisted suicide are concerned with individual rights and the suffering endured by terminally ill patients. The debates surrounding each of these issues are complex, and often individuals who support one of these issues do not support all three.

Thus, while many pro-life groups found the pope's condemnation of the "culture of death" apt, some religious leaders criticized "The Gospel of Life" for failing to consider the varying views held by supporters of abortion, assisted suicide, and the death penalty. Many worried that by classifying them all as part of a broad "culture of death," the pope appeared inflexible and confrontational, and made public discourse about these issues more divisive. The editors of *Commonweal* magazine write that "judging modern democracy uniquely depraved is neither plausible nor persuasive." Instead, they argue, society must go beyond the "life vs. death" mentality and begin a meaningful dialogue on these issues:

> In rightly defending the "absolute" value of human life, the pope's rhetoric and style do not fully acknowledge the complexity of the political situation. Individual rights and personal autonomy are the philosophical bedrock of Western society. Abortion and euthanasia are particularly difficult questions because they cut to the heart of the endlessly negotiated relationship between self-determination and social or moral duty.

The abortion debate, the right-to-die movement, and the morality of capital punishment have and will continue to be emotionally charged issues, precisely because they so often touch on questions of life and death. The Catholic Church's teachings on these issues have been fundamental in shaping the modern debate over these "problems of death." *Problems of Death: Opposing Viewpoints* offers a study of this debate in the following chapters: Is Suicide Immoral? Should Society Condone Physician-Assisted Suicide? Is Abortion Ethical? Is Capital Punishment Just? The essays that follow are intended to introduce the reader to the broad range of ethical questions surrounding death.

CHAPTER 1

Is Suicide Immoral?

Chapter Preface

The morality of suicide is an issue that has divided philosophers for centuries. The ancient Romans, for example, seem to have held the credo of "death before dishonor" in high regard. Two of history's most famous suicides are those of Anthony and Cleopatra, who took their own lives after their forces were defeated at the Battle of Actium in 31 B.C. The Roman statesman Brutus also committed suicide after a military defeat, and Cato the Younger took his own life to protest Julius Caesar's dictatorship of Rome.

At first glance, the argument that these suicides were moral seem simple enough: Unlike murderers, suicidal individuals cause direct harm to no one but themselves, and they do so willingly. In this view, the decision to die rather than to degrade oneself before an enemy might be seen as ennobling. However, throughout history, widespread acceptance of suicide has been the exception rather than the rule for a variety of reasons.

Most Christian traditions regard suicide as the destruction of innocent life, and thus a sin. Legal scholars have argued that one purpose of government is to prevent all killing, whether it be through homicide or suicide. Some ethicists have argued that, instead of being courageous, suicide is a cowardly response to life's adversities. Others maintain that suicide is wrong because of the harm it causes to friends, families, and the community as a whole. Mental health professionals often oppose self-killing on the grounds that suicidal tendencies are a sign of mental illness.

No doubt all of these views have contributed to modern taboos about suicide. However, the diverse arguments concerning the morality of suicide continue to spark debate among ethicists. In the subsequent chapter, modern ethicists critique many of the classic arguments concerning suicide made by renowned thinkers such as Aristotle, Thomas Aquinas, and David Hume. The authors of the following viewpoints also offer some of their own reasons to condone or condemn suicide.

> *"We all have an instinctive wish to continue living. But instincts leave us some choice, allowing reason to direct our actions, sometimes in defiance of our instincts."*

Suicide Should Be an Individual Choice

Ernest van den Haag

In the following viewpoint, Ernest van den Haag argues that there is no reason why mentally competent persons should not be allowed to end their lives if they so choose. He rejects both religious and philosophical objections to suicide, and maintains that it is only humans' basic instinct to survive that has led them to condemn the idea of willfully choosing death. Van den Haag is a psychoanalyst and retired professor of jurisprudence and public policy.

As you read, consider the following questions:
1. What is van den Haag's response to the argument that suicidal people must suffer from a mental disorder?
2. According to van den Haag, why did Aristotle oppose suicide?
3. What is the key difference between murder and suicide, in the author's opinion?

Excerpted from "Why Does Suicide Have a Bad Reputation?" by Ernest van den Haag, *Chronicles*, August 1998. Reprinted with permission from *Chronicles*. This article does not necessarily reflect the views of *Chronicles* or its editors.

Whether and when we enter this world is decided not by, but for us. Nor is it up to us to decide when to leave it. Most of us would like to stay longer than we are allowed—but our lifespan is ordained by forces beyond our control. We are quite resigned to this; however, when we become greatly impaired and life no longer holds much promise, some of us think of shortening it and of asking others to help if necessary. Is that legitimate? Are there serious moral objections?

Religious Objections to Suicide

In the past, the usual lifespan was brief and illness often ended it abruptly. The old were honored largely because they were so few. We live longer now, and death is likely to approach gradually, depriving us of our abilities one by one, until we sink into incompetence and finally unconsciousness. This has made shortening life more tempting. Yet most people feel that they ought to be no more responsible for their death than they were for their birth. Religion and tradition also tell us that we ought to wait patiently for our end and always try to postpone, never to advance it. The medical profession sees this as its main task, and most non-physicians as well think it presumptuous to engineer death ourselves. It might be premature in any case: unforeseen good things may still be in store. No animal commits suicide, and our animal instincts oppose it. Thus we are resigned to a natural death, the date not chosen by us, or known in advance.

But instinct, religion, and tradition do not always prevail. There would be no problem if they did. Suicides do occur, even though most people look upon them with horror, as an aberration explainable only by madness. Indeed, there frequently is a mental disorder; but not always. And the assumption that mental disorder *ipso facto* must be the cause of suicide conveniently avoids moral problems that ought to be addressed.

The pre-Christian ancients, perhaps with the exception of the Stoics, did not favor suicide. But they opposed it only mildly, thinking it reasonable at least in some situations and obligatory in others. However, the Judeo-Christian religion fervently opposes suicide, although there is no scriptural warrant for this opposition: the Bible nowhere condemns suicide. Yet the traditional opposition seldom is questioned even by those alienated from tradition. It rests on the belief that God created us in His image and endowed us with many abilities, including free will. We are the Creator's creatures. He gave us life—and He alone has the right to take it. We do not. "Thy will be done."

Under certain circumstances, others may lawfully and with divine sanction kill us, but we never are allowed to do so ourselves. Life is a gift from God, and it would be irreverent and impious to throw it away. Above all, our life is not ours to dispose of. We are but stewards entrusted with God's property. In some ways this view makes life appear as though a prison. God holds the key, and we are morally bound to stay until released. In due time He will let us out to go to heaven or to hell. Meanwhile, attempts to escape by climbing over the walls are illegitimate and sinful and will be punished accordingly. Yet we did not volunteer for life. Whether we can legitimately volunteer for death is the problem—at least for the non-religious.

Philosophical Arguments Against Suicide

Philosophical arguments against suicide are neither cheerful nor persuasive. Aristotle thought that in many ways we are creatures of the communities that reared us and have a duty to live so that we may contribute to them. This is an uncommonly weak argument. It would follow that, should we become a burden on the community, suicide would become legitimate, perhaps even required. (Aristotle does not draw this inference.) Further, whatever the community did for us, we never volunteered to join it and to become obligated to live when we no longer want to. In modern times, involuntary obligations are always questionable, although most people recognize some such obligations, e.g., to their parents. An involuntary natural obligation to live may be analogously constructed. We also may be morally obligated to obey laws for which we did not volunteer. But laws prohibiting such things as murder or fraud protect us from one another, whereas the prohibition of suicide would protect us from ourselves. This does not seem to be called for. It is unclear to whom the obligation to live is owed and how it is justified. Aristotle further thought that suicide violates "right reason" and therefore is "unjust" toward nature and the state. Plato, too, opposed suicide without offering much of an argument. He writes, "A person who kills himself [is] violently robbing what fate has allotted," without bothering to argue the authority of fate. Why must we obey it when we can do otherwise?

John Locke decided that we own the product of our labor because "every man has a property in his own person" and, therefore, in whatever he produces. It would be a small step to infer that, since we own ourselves, we can dispose of ourselves and decide whether to live or die. Property, after all, is the right to dispose of what one owns. But, being a good Christian, Locke did not take this step. We remain God's creatures and owe a duty to live the life God gave us. "Everyone is bound to preserve himself and not to quit his station willfully." In effect, we don't fully own ourselves (contrary to what libertarians believe) but merely are in (temporary) possession, tenants on God's property.

A Duty to Live?

Immanuel Kant opposed suicide as a violation of the duty to live. He thought we owe this duty to ourselves. But a duty owed by and to ourselves is not very different from a debt owed by and to ourselves—which we can always forgive. Actually, since the debtor and the creditor are the same person, no debt is really owed to anyone by anyone. To say that we owe a debt, or a duty, to ourselves means no more than that we feel we ought to do (or not to do) something. It adds no argument, only emphasis, to that feeling, while suggesting that an independent argument has been added. In the words of Thomas Hobbes: "He that can bind can release; and therefore he that is bound to himself only, is not bound."

The notion of a duty owed to oneself also may envision a split in the self between a part to which the duty is owed and the part owing it. Such internal conflicts do occur (without them psychotherapists could not make a living). Quite possibly, conscience (or our long-term interest) wants one thing and the pleasure-seeking part of the self another. Still, the duty to which conscience calls us is always a duty either to others or to some moral idea which we have accepted. Kant thought that our duty is to reason. (But he did not show that suicide is irrational.) The obligatoriness of the duty depends on the moral weight of its demands, not on its being a duty to oneself. And Kant did not actually offer a convincing argument for the duty to live.

Dying for an Ideal

I believe that suicide is justifiable in defense of one's ideals, one's beliefs, one's values. . . .

Sam Henry's entire life had been spent on or in the close vicinity of a small river. He was on that river from his earliest memories through every one of his life's most significant events. He met a young lass on the river and courted her on it. After marriage and the birth of their only child he built a house on that river and all three continued to live on it.

In later years, after their daughter had married and moved out, after 40 years of a marriage devoted to each other, he had what they called a "stroke." Afterwards, he could no longer devote himself to his wife, his daughter and her husband, the work at the mill, or even to his boat. He could not tie his own shoes, feed himself, or even tell his wife what he wanted to eat. After a year of trying various therapies to no avail, he went down to that river he loved and shot himself. The ideal he thus defended was the person he would be; had been for so long. He did not prefer death but accepted it rather than continue a living death. Sam Henry's death was heroic; it was accepted in defense of ideals. It is not something anyone should condemn.

Samuel E. Wallace, "The Moral Imperative to Suicide," in James L. Werth, ed., *Contemporary Perspectives on Rational Suicide*. Philadelphia: Brunner/Mazel, 1999.

Arthur Schopenhauer did not think highly of life. He was convinced that the suffering it brings exceeds its pleasures. (He did not tell how he measured and compared.) Since desire brings suffering in excess of the pleasure of fulfillment, Schopenhauer felt that we should strive for desirelessness, as he believed Hindus and Buddhists did. Thus, by avoiding life (for to avoid desire is to avoid life), we would avoid suffering. One might think that Schopenhauer would justify suicide, but he actually opposed it as an illegitimate means of achieving desirelessness. Buddhists thought that suicide would only bring reincarnation, not Nirvana. Schopenhauer's arguments seem unusually murky here. But one must remember that, by justifying suicide, philosophers would place themselves in an awkward position: they would have to justify staying alive while arguing in favor of being dead if they argued that suicide is obligatory, or even desirable. Schopenhauer preferred to make it attractive (or to make life unattractive) but futile. Among major philosophers, David Hume was alone in thinking suicide legitimate. He has remained alone.

Suicide Should Be Discouraged but Not Prohibited

Few people want to commit suicide and every effort should be made to dissuade them, for their wish may be temporary. However, if they are altogether resolved, they cannot be prevented at length from carrying out their intention, and if they are mentally competent, there is no justification for thwarting them. There is no justification either for denying help to those who, although mentally competent, are physically so disabled that they need and request help to end their life. Their wish for ending their life is more intelligible than that of others. But no excuse is needed from a secular viewpoint. It is your life to end or to continue.

Why do so many people insist that suicide always ought to be prevented even when preventing it prolongs the hopeless suffering of incurably sick persons? Why does suicide horrify people? Chaste persons not only abstain from illicit sex, but also usually think that those who do not are morally wrong (or at least weak) and should be prevented from doing what they want. That is also how people who want to live feel about people who want to die. Could it be, then, that we feel that those who do not act according to the survival instinct we all share are, as it were, traitors to life, quitters who give in to a temptation that must be shunned, even though (or perhaps because) it is felt at times by nearly everyone?

Murdering others is wrong and a crime because it takes the life of those who were entitled to live and did not want to die. But suicide ends the life of a person who no longer wishes to live. He obviously consents to taking his own life, or to having it taken. What makes killing others wrong, what makes homicide murder, is lack of consent. Consensual intercourse is legitimate, but non-consensual intercourse is rape and a crime. The law acknowledges the difference which consent makes with regard to sex (and to property) but ignores it with regard to homicide, including assisted suicide, perhaps because consent cannot be valid if (as religious dogma asserts) we don't own ourselves; more likely because consensual intercourse (or property transfer) is common, whereas consensual homicide certainly is not.

Allowing Individuals to Control Their Lifespan

We all have an instinctive wish to continue living. But instincts leave us some choice, allowing reason to direct our actions, sometimes in defiance of our instincts. Unlike animals, we have a choice, and can act according to our moral norms. Yet the prevailing hostility to suicide and its infamous reputation have led our society to cruel and immoral policies. We threaten to punish anyone, including physicians, who helps another to end his life.

There are dangers in legalizing assisted suicide or euthanasia, mainly concerning competent and informed consent. But these dangers can be surmounted by appropriate precautions. Once we discard the presumption (actually a circular definition) that all persons bent on suicide *ipso facto* are insane, we have to make sure that those requesting assistance are mentally competent. Some objectors insist that this can never be reliably ascertained. This seems absurd. Laymen as well as psychiatrists are quite capable of distinguishing persons of sound mind from others who, temporarily or permanently, are not. Were it not so, valid contracts or wills could never be made, and no business could be done. It is bizarre to argue that we can distinguish the sane from the insane except when it comes to people who wish to die. The possibility of abuse which bedevils all human practices can never be eliminated altogether, but safeguards can minimize abuse. To argue that physicians, once they are authorized to help those who request help to end their life, would also shorten the life of people who wanted to live is no better than arguing that once physicians are authorized to amputate diseased limbs, they will amputate healthy ones as well. No slope is that slippery.

Why does suicide have such a bad reputation? It defies what we instinctively feel and want to believe: that life is always worth living, whatever the circumstances. It seems to reject life itself and thereby to breach the solidarity of the living. Without this solidarity, there can be no society. Human solidarity, cultivated by religious, political, and educational institutions, takes many forms. But those who breach it by suicide are always seen as renegades. They used to be ostracized even in death. Plato urged that they be interred in "isolated" graves. In the Middle Ages, they were denied consecrated ground, and a stake was driven through their hearts. Yet some cultures have made allowances for suicide. It has not endangered their societies. Suicide is not infectious (despite occasional imitations), and it is unlikely ever to become popular enough to endanger any society. Nothing is lost, then, if we stop hindering or prohibiting assistance. Something is gained. We will, at last, allow individuals to control their lifespan within the boundaries set by nature, and we will reduce or eliminate the immense undeserved suffering to which hitherto we have sentenced so many innocent people.

*"Suicide is . . . not a private act at all. . . .
We are models for each other's lives, even if
we think we are not."*

Suicide Should Not Be a Matter of Individual Choice

Daniel Callahan

In the following viewpoint, Daniel Callahan contends that in a liberal society, individuals have the freedom to do whatever they want so long as their choices do not harm others. However, Callahan believes that the act of suicide does harm others, because it represents a rejection of the bonds that hold people together in the face of life's adversities. He concludes that while individual suicides should be pitied rather than condemned, suicide in general should not be considered a legitimate way of dealing with pain and suffering. Callahan is a philosopher, cofounder and former president of the medical ethics organization the Hastings Center, and author of many books, including *The Troubled Dream of Life: In Search of a Peaceful Death.*

As you read, consider the following questions:
1. Why does Callahan believe that people generally feel a sense of loss and pity when someone commits suicide?
2. According to Callahan, some suicide advocates argue for suicide in cases of "excessive or meaningless" suffering, but not "ordinary" suffering. What are the author's objections to this position?
3. In the author's view, what "tolerable balance" has society reached in regard to suicide?

Excerpted from "Reasons, Rationality, and Ways of Life," by Daniel Callahan, in *Contemporary Perspectives on Rational Suicide*, edited by James L. Werth (Philadelphia: Brunner/Mazel, 1999). Copyright ©1999 by Taylor & Francis. Reprinted with permission from Taylor & Francis.

It seems utterly unhelpful to note that many religions have strictures against suicide and thereby classify opposition to suicide as religious. The more interesting issue is why quite diverse religions and societies have taken that position.

Human Solidarity in the Face of Adversity

I offer a hypothesis, one that seems to me a good moral argument. The general repugnance most societies, and religions, have to suicide stems from the perception that it represents a profound failure to cope with life. But it is a social and not just individual failure: it breaks the solidarity that people should have in the face of the evils and tragedies of life. Almost all lives will have to face the death of loved ones, the pain and suffering of illness, occupational failures and reverses, family misery, and—in the most extreme cases— wars, massacres, persecution, and unleashed savagery. Life at its worst offers us many reasons to be rid of it, and most people will at some time in their lives think of suicide as a tempting escape, definitive and final.

Why do most people not give in to that temptation? Perhaps, as is sometimes alleged, it is a fear of the act of suicide, or superstition, or an unwillingness to take one's rational conclusions to their final stage. However, I suspect it is because we have been socially tutored that, despite pain, suffering, and tragedy, life ought to go on, and that we owe it to each other not to despair in the face of evil and misfortune. We are implicitly asked by our fellow human beings to give witness to the possibility of human endurance and the need to transcend evil by bearing it in our own lives. We need the help of other people in coping with what life throws our way, and one of the most fundamental goods that others can give us is the example of their lives in enduring pain and misery. If others can do it, so can I. And if I cannot do it, I will thereby be failing in my duty to others, failing to give them the kind of help that they, by simply enduring, have given me. One reason why we typically feel a sense of loss and pity when someone commits suicide is because we guess that the person has not only chosen to leave life, but also to leave the human community in a way that does some harm to those of us who remain: the harm of someone who could not find out how to maintain solidarity with us in the presence of pain and suffering.

For all of the evident advantages of suicide, most otherwise rational people do not choose it as a way of managing their lives and their sorrows. No doubt there is a powerful drive for life, a desire just to stay alive, that is operating here. It probably has deep biological roots, a way of coping with the various threats to life, whether social or biological. The uniqueness of human beings among other creatures is that they can contemplate, and carry out, fantasies about being dead and thus being rid of their burdens. Yet comparatively few act on those fantasies. Most interestingly as well, the pain, suffering, tragedies, and disappointments of life are not good predictors of who will attempt or actually commit suicide. Most people are able to tolerate the evils of life without committing suicide: even the severely handicapped, on the one hand, and those imprisoned in inhuman concentration camps, on the other, rarely commit suicide. They just do not take that way out even if a terrible ending awaits them. Most people who are dying, even if they are undergoing great pain, do not request much less pursue suicide. . . .

Rational Versus Moral Choices

Now there is not, so far as I can see, any public and articulated tradition of suicide as a way of life in our society. There does, however, seem to be a kind of prototradition, part of the ethos of a liberal society, that some people apply to suicide. That tradition holds that competent individuals may make whatever moral choices they want, including suicide, if there is no demonstrable harm to others. A reasonable choice in this tradition is one that is compatible with a person's values and self-perceived interests, *whatever* they might be. At the least, the choice should be rational (internally coherent and consistent), but at most it will qualify as reasonable if the person has thought long and hard about it and can offer, to himself or herself, some defensible justification. It is not the job of society, in this tradition, to determine what counts as a reasonable way of life, or defensible premises for committing suicide.

I believe that this tradition is simply wrong (not irrational), unconscionably thin, and relativistic. It is not enough to put forward an individualistic, formalistic kind of response, and then to say that suicide is reasonable if it is compatible with a person's values and self-perceived interests. That repeats the ultimate failing of those criteria for "rational" suicide that rest, in a wholly circular manner, on the premise that an act is acceptably rational if consistent with the actor's self-perceived interests. That just takes us back to the trivial sense of rationality, that of interior consistency and coherence. In this case, to determine whether suicide is a reasonable act must be to determine whether it is *actually* in people's interest—because they can be mistaken to think it is—and whether it is *actually* in the interest of society to see it legitimated as a reasonable option for those who choose it.

The only good way to get at the question of what is really in our interest is to ask ourselves whether we want to be the kind of people who believe suicide to be reasonable and to live in the kind of society that thinks it is? I argue that no one should want to become that kind of person, and that no one should want to live in such a society. At the same time, we should be willing to understand and empathize with those who, not as a way of life but as a desperate and singular act, commit suicide in the face of severe travail. We should all be able to understand why that can happen, but we should no less be able to understand why we do not want to legitimate such acts as a standard part of our way of life.

Examining One's Fundamental Values

In light of the problem of suicide, how might I go about deciding what kind of person I ought to be, and whether I ought to let myself become the kind of person for whom suicide is a legitimate option? I would want to begin by trying to determine how I should evaluate the pain and suffering that might come into my life. If I choose to be the kind of person who simply tolerates no severe suffering that might be remotely avoidable, then suicide will look attractive. If I also believe that I ought to be the kind of person who can control life as far as is possible, accepting nothing that is not self-chosen, then suicide will look even more attractive. If I believe that it ought to be me, and not my society, that determines what counts as intolerable suffering, then suicide will have gained a few more points in my eyes. Finally, if I can persuade myself that suicide is truly a private act, of no consequence to those around me (assuming I have discharged any formal obligations I might have to them before committing suicide), then my own case for suicide will have been nicely made.

Suicide Is a Symptom of Social Disconnect

In his classic study *Suicide*, Durkheim wondered why suicide rates have risen so sharply in modern industrial societies. His answer was to propose his theory of anomie, which is the sense of being personally unconnected to others, not being in a web of what the contemporary anthropologist Clifford Geertz has called "thick" culture. It is the sense of loneliness that comes upon people when they are increasingly taken by others and themselves as dispensable producers and consumers. In such a cold, uncaring environment, more and more desperate people sense that their own lives are simply more than they can bear by themselves alone.

David Novak, *First Things*, August/September 1997.

But I might choose to be another kind of person. I could perceive that a good part of life requires bearing pain and suffering and that, although it may never be good in itself, the price of trying to evade it at every turn can be a high one, limiting my possibilities for flourishing and fulfillment. A life based on the negative value of the avoidance of suffering would seem a thin and defensive kind of life. But stop. In the case of rational and reasonable suicide, are we not talking mainly about undue or excessive or meaningless suffering, not the ordinary suffering that comes with living a life? Not necessarily, for if we want to leave it to individuals to determine what counts as excessive or meaningless—that is, to have no substantive standards at all—we open the door to judging even ordinary suffering as unacceptable. . . . The step from a desire to be relieved of suffering to the averting of suffering is a short one.

I have hypothesized in this chapter that one of the reasons why most societies have refused to legitimate suicide as a routine way to relieve suffering is because of the need for solidarity in the face of suffering. We somehow ought to show each other that we can bear what life throws in our path in order that we each may better bear it. I need the witness of my neighbor that pain can be borne just as she or he needs the same witness on my part. If we are essentially social creatures, not simply isolated moral monads, then our life with other people will affect the way we look at life: we will learn from them just as they will learn from us. Suicide is, in that respect, not a private act at all: families have to live with its aftermath, even as do those who merely collect the bodies of those who have committed suicide. We are models for each other's lives, even if we think we are not. A society that legitimated suicide as a way of life would be creating a wholly different set of models: those who choose to reject the older tradition of solidarity in favor of a more contemporary tradition of self-determination and the evasion of suffering.

Actually, I think our present situation, in which suicide has not been legitimated as a reasonable way of coping with suffering, but in which individual suicides are rarely condemned, is a good one. We have reached a tolerable balance between a resistance to suicide as a way of life and routine death, and its acceptance on rare occasions as the sad, desperate act of someone stretched beyond his or her limits. We feel pity and sorrow and sometimes perplexity at such a death and we hesitate to pass moral judgment. That seems to me a good balance. But the pressure now is to disturb that balance, to see the moral status of suicide elevated, attitudes toward suffering and the sharing of suffering altered, and the idea of rational suicide used to imply that, if the minimal test of rationality can be established, then the case for suicide has de facto been made. It has, however, not been thereby made. I have offered here only the most cursory sketch of another way of thinking about suicide, by trying to goad people to think about how they *ought* to live their own lives (not just what their "interests" are); and by getting society to ask what kind of a community it wants to be.

> *"It is not immediately clear just how the suicide injures the community of which he or she is part."*

Suicide Does Not Always Harm Society

Margaret Pabst Battin

Margaret Pabst Battin is a philosophy professor at the University of Utah. In her book *Ethical Issues in Suicide*, she contends that suicide can be a rational act, and that the government has no right to prohibit mentally competent individuals from ending their lives. In the following excerpt from that book, she responds to several classical arguments that suicide harms society by causing grief to family members, depriving the community of the good an individual might still do, and inciting others to commit suicide. Battin contends that although these arguments may be used to prove that a specific individual's suicide is wrong, they do not support a blanket prohibition on all suicide.

As you read, consider the following questions:

1. What example does Battin give to demonstrate her view that the special-talents argument against suicide is a highly elitist one?
2. At what point in a person's life did Charlotte Perkins Gilman, as quoted by the author, consider suicide permissible?
3. In Battin's opinion, what does the deprivation-of-good argument fail to consider?

A ristotle is widely acknowledged as the originator of the view that suicide damages society. In the *Nicomachean Ethics*, he claims that the individual who destroys himself is "treating the state unjustly," and that therefore criminal sanctions against the suicide are appropriate.

> . . . he who through anger voluntarily stabs himself does this contrary to the right rule of life, and this the law does not allow; therefore he is acting unjustly. But towards whom? Surely towards the state, not towards himself. For he suffers voluntarily, but no one is voluntarily treated unjustly. This is also the reason why the state punishes; a certain loss of civil rights attaches to the man who destroys himself, on the ground that he is treating the state unjustly.

Inspection of the context surrounding this passage will reveal that Aristotle makes his remark on suicide parenthetically, as an illustration of his theory of just and unjust behavior. Nevertheless, the notion he puts forward of suicide as an "injury to the state" is accepted by a great many later writers on suicide. For Thomas Aquinas it is another of the three principal reasons why suicide is wrong:

> Second, every part belongs to the whole in virtue of what it is. But every man is part of the community, so that he belongs to the community in virtue of what he is. Suicide therefore involves damaging the community, as Aristotle makes clear.

. . . This notion is taken to supply the theoretical basis upon which legal sanctions and punishment can be imposed: Since suicide damages the state, suicide prohibitions, and punishments for attempted, assisted, and even completed suicide, are justified.

Yet it is not immediately clear just how the suicide injures the community of which he or she is part. . . .

Suicide as an Injury to Family and Friends

The suicide of an individual may have serious and painful effects on his or her immediate family and friends. It causes grief and emotional pain; it may also cause other distress, such as the economic deprivation incurred if the victim was the central supporter of the family. It may deprive children of a parent, a spouse of conjugal companionship, and friends, acquaintances, and fellow workers of the benefits and pleasures of association with the victim. Some of these effects may be more severe and more damaging than others, but in general, suicide can cause deep grief and deprivation to family and friends.

This is a familiar argument against suicide, one that we take very seriously. . . .

The general argument that suicide causes injury to one's family or friends is disputed in several classic ways. Some authors have claimed that although suicide may cause grief and harm to one's family or friends, it is no worse than desertion, and thus not an evil of greater degree. Others have pointed out that although suicide does often cause such harm, some people have no family or friends who would be affected by their suicide. Finally, it is often suggested that the harm is essentially transitory; Landsberg remarks that "everyone dies sooner or later, and society and the family get over it.". . . .

But this is to treat somewhat cavalierly a point that should be treated with extreme gravity and circumspection. An individual's suicide can cause more than a simple episode of grief or a limited period of pain in the people he or she leaves behind; it can ruin their lives. . . . Most importantly the fact of suicide adds a new component of guilt to ordinary grief: Since suicide is an act often resulting from extreme unhappiness and stress, the survivor will tend to see himself or herself as having had a central role in producing that unhappiness and stress. "What did I do wrong?" or "Why did I make her do it?" are perhaps the simplest expressions of the grief/guilt constellation that death by suicide engenders in survivors; its manifestions can be considerably more complex. The guilt response may be based on a faulty picture of one's own role and importance in the victim's life, or it may accurately betray one's own causal role in producing the suicide. Either way, this guilt is often ruinous and absolute, as in the case of a parent whose only child has committed suicide, or the spouse of a suicided mate. Counseling of the survivors may help, but even with counseling, the psychological damage to the survivor may be extensive and sometimes permanent.

The effects are not entirely psychological either. There are many other forms of damage that suicide may render to the survivors: for instance, legal, financial, and insurance-associated difficulties, as well as readjustment and job-related difficulties rooted in ostracism by one's social or religious group. This ostracism, which may have both psychological and economic effects, is itself exacerbated by the tacit but pervasive assumption that family members and other close associates must have had some covert causal role in the victim's suicide. They may be thought to have responsibility for the suicide by indirect or coercive suggestion, by insensitivity to warnings, or by simply having made the victim's life so miserable that she saw no other choice. Whether justified or not, the ostracism of a suicide survivor often constitutes a severe hardship; coupled with genuine grief and with practical difficulties, it can be ruinous. It is almost impossible to overestimate the impact suicide can have on other, especially closely related, individuals.

The Stigma Attached to Suicide
Causes More Harm than Suicide Itself

Nevertheless, even the likelihood of ruinous impact does not argue adequately against the moral permissibility of suicide in general. The severe grief/guilt constellation among survivors occurs only in a society in which suicide is believed wrong, and most strongly in a society in which not only the practice but the discussion of suicide is under heavy taboo. This has certainly been true of present Western society, though it is changing; but it is not true of all. In Stoic Rome, for instance, suicide was thought to be a noble kind of death, the free choice of an enlightened human being; it occasioned grief but no guilt; ideally, it brought admiration. In our society the suicide of their child is almost certain to cause severe grief and guilt to the surviving parents, but this is not always the case in suicide-permissive societies. Consider, for instance, Seneca's description of the suicide of a Spartan youth, and the reactions he indicates a parent should have:

> History relates the story of the famous Spartan, a mere boy who, when he was taken prisoner, kept shouting in his native Doric, "I shall not be a slave!" He was as good as his word. The first time he was ordered to perform a slave's task, some humiliating household job (his actual orders were to fetch a disgusting chamber pot), he dashed his head against a wall and cracked his skull open. Freedom is as near as that—is

anyone really still a slave? Would you not rather your own son died like that than lived by reason of spinelessness to an advanced age?

. . . In the earlier periods of Western history, in both Greece and apparently also in the early Hebrew communities, suicide was not thought intrinsically wrong. Consequently the particular grief/guilt constellation so damaging to suicide survivors in our society most probably did not occur, or did not occur to such a degree. What did occur was normal, genuine grief over a death. . . . The severity of the psychological damage that suicides in our present society produce in the survivors is not to be underrated; on the contrary, we tend to treat it much too lightly. But that such damage occurs does not show that suicide is in itself morally wrong; what we see, rather, is that the damage may be very largely the product of our own society's pervasive belief that suicide is seriously wrong.

Suicide as the Deprivation of an Individual's Contribution to Society

Although not every suicide causes harm to particular individuals among family, friends, or immediate associates, it may still be the case that suicide does harm the society as a whole. Among the oldest arguments of this sort—arising not only from Aristotle but from Plato before him—is that which considers the suicide to be depriving the community, state, or social group of his or her labor or other contribution to its welfare. . . .

Even in a society that is not highly mutually interdependent, some individuals' contributions of labor or services to the society may be unique and nonreplaceable, or may involve skills that are in shortage or for which substitutions cannot easily be made: One might mention the physician in a small town, the highly talented musician or artist, the key scientist, diplomat, and so forth. In this case, because the labor of individuals with unique gifts or crucial skills cannot be replaced, the suicide of such individuals would deprive society of a considerable need and good. . . .

Nevertheless, it is still not clear that the deprivation-of-special-talents argument succeeds as an argument against suicide even for those who have irreplaceable special talents and whose talents and skills remain intact. The argument against suicide is really an argument against failure to exercise those talents; consequently, it will be applicable not only to suicide but also to other actions that would deprive society of these special services or labor. But it is not evident that we consider this position correct with respect to other actions; for instance, we do not prevent the physician from leaving a practice to change professions or to join a monastery, and we do not force musicians or dancers or actors to continue to perform. . . . To be consistent, we should consider the suicide of a skilled physician more wrong than that of a master chessplayer; the suicide of a car-wash attendant would not be wrong at all. The special-talents argument is thus a highly elitist one. It presents only a very weak case against suicide, prohibiting it in only those individuals whose contributions are highly valued and unique. . . .

The Deprivation-of-Good Argument

The ["deprivation-of-good"] argument is simply this: One ought not commit suicide if one can, alternatively, do good; suicide is wrong because it deprives society of whatever good an individual might do. . . .

No doubt the most eloquent defender of the deprivation-of-good argument against suicide has been Charlotte Perkins Gilman, the labor and women's-rights activist of the early part of the twentieth century. She writes as follows:

> A last duty. Human life consists in mutual service. No grief, no pain, misfortune or "broken heart" is excuse for cutting off one's life while any power of service remains.

Gilman offers no support for the central premise in this argument, that "human life consists in mutual service." Whether such a premise is provided by utilitarian or by other ethical theories is, of course, a much-debated issue: Do we have a positive obligation to do good, or simply a negative obligation to refrain from harm?

But there is a second question here: Even if we could establish that human beings have a positive obligation to do good, would this serve as the basis of a general argument against suicide? For Gilman it does not. The words just quoted are taken from Gilman's suicide note, written as she was afflicted with terminal cancer. They continue:

> ... But when all usefulness is over, when one is assured of an imminent and unavoidable death, it is the simplest of human rights to choose a quick and easy death in place of a slow and horrible one. Public opinion is changing on this subject. The time is approaching when we shall consider it abhorrent to our civilization to allow a human being to lie in prolonged agony which we should mercifully end in any other creature. Believing this choice to be of social service in promoting wiser views on this question, I have preferred chloroform to cancer.

Gilman assumes that her "usefulness" or power of doing good will be lost to medical dependency, pain, and the disruption of social relationships that terminal illness often produces, and that consequently the obligation to do good is no bar to suicide in these circumstances. Is her view correct? Popular medical literature is filled with tales of heroic individuals who have done astonishing good from their iron lungs or their respirators or their quadriplegic wheelchairs, and of people who even in the intense suffering of their dying moments have served as an inspiration to others; this might suggest that Gilman's view that suicide is morally permitted in the face of oncoming death, since one can no longer do good, is wrong. But it is not clear that the deprivation-of-good argument, even if such accounts are accepted, will speak against the permissibility of suicide even where the individual could continue to do good. The deprivation-of-good argument does not consider the degree to which satisfaction of the individual's own interests may be outweighed by the obligation to do good. The principle that individuals have an obligation to do good is not one of utter self-sacrifice, and we might find it morally odd to insist that persons do good at the cost of severe harm to themselves. Someone whose life has already reached such excesses of misery that he or she is considering ending it would hardly be obligated to continue that misery-filled life in order to do good for others—especially when doing good for others carries no guarantee of improving his or her own condition and may even worsen it. Certainly different ethical theories will weigh this balance in different ways; the utilitarian, for instance, may believe that the individual is obligated to continue to live and do good despite any suffering when the amount of good he or she can do is very large; other theories may resolve this issue in quite different ways. But this is the issue that must be resolved before we can determine whether the deprivation-of-good argument is successful against suicide in those cases in which suicide is most likely to be contemplated—namely those in which human misery is greatest.

The Severely Disabled

A variant of the argument from doing good maintains that the collective presence of severely disabled or defective individuals contributes good to society even though the individuals themselves do not perform good acts or actively do good in any other way. Here the good contributed by such individuals inheres in the responses of others to them, not in any actions of their own, and it is this good that precludes their suicides. For instance, the violinist who contracts a degenerative disease and loses the use of his hands nevertheless continues to do good, though he can no longer contribute his violin-playing services to society and though he directly performs no other morally good acts, by becoming the object of the moral intentions of others. The victim takes no active role, but functions as a kind of whetstone upon which those not afflicted may sharpen their moral feelings. Since the exercise of moral feelings is a good, which the afflicted person makes possible, he ought not end this opportunity by suicide. David Novak, discussing St. Thomas Aquinas, expresses such a view; it is prevalent in a wide variety of religious and nonreligious sources. Novak writes:

> . . . one can see a need for even the helpless and infirm. Their very presence enables us to practice the human virtues of benevolence and generosity.

Of all the social arguments against suicide, this may be one of the most disturbing. It may be true that contact with debilitated, disabled, deformed, or otherwise distressed persons does intensify our moral feelings and does give rise to greater sympathy, benevolence, and caring for other persons in general. Such persons may serve as inspiring models and may make us more courageous in enduring our own afflictions. But to claim that those persons have an *obligation* to live (and suffer) in order to make normal individuals more

39

humane or courageous is ethically questionable at best. One might also see it as a barbaric holdover of earlier European practices, according to which caged lunatics were placed on public display, criminals put in public stocks, and physically anomalous persons were displayed in circuses, presumably for the moral edification as well as entertainment of individuals not so afflicted. It is not at all obvious that we should sanction an argument that, in essence, argues that the helpless and infirm have an obligation to submit to similar treatment—to refrain from suicide, even though they would choose it, and instead remain alive as objects for our pity and moral elevation. . . .

The Problem of Universal Suicide

If large numbers of individuals—even ordinary individuals without special talents—were to withdraw their labor, services, or good-doing from society by suicide, the function of the whole might be seriously impaired. This would certainly constitute an "injury to society." While the possibility of widespread suicide may seem remote, there is some historical evidence that it has been considered a threat at various times. For instance, the Roman legal sanctions against suicide, which applied only to slaves and to soldiers on duty, were apparently designed to prevent widespread suicide among groups whose labor was considered critical. John Donne implies that strong suicide prohibitions serve to ensure the availability of the laboring class.

> . . . yet the number of wretched men exceeds the happy (for every laborer is miserable and beastlike, in respect of the idle, abounding men). It was therefore thought necessary, by laws and by opinion of religion . . . to take from these weary and macerated wretches their ordinary and open escape and ease, voluntary death.

. . . But even an assumption like Donne's that the possibility of mass self-extinction is undesirable and hence is grounds for a general policy against suicide is open to philosophic question. One could argue that not even widespread suicide constitutes an injury to society. Indeed some thinkers appear to welcome the prospect of widespread suicide. Though little is known of his exact views, Hegesias the Cyrenaic is said to have preached a doctrine recommending suicide so effectively that Ptolemy II was forced to put a stop to his teachings. Schopenhauer advocates the overcoming of the will to live, though this, he says, cannot be accomplished by ordinary suicide, and only rarely through self-starvation. Eduard von Hartmann argues that instead of private, individual suicide, all humankind—having continued to suffer and to achieve a common awareness that life is essentially evil and futile—must join together and, in a common act of will, decree their own extinction; this is universal, simultaneous suicide, designed to rid the world of an unpleasant and unsuccessful form of life. These views may seem bizarre. But even if we assume that universal suicide would be wrong, this of course does not suffice to show that individual acts of suicide are so.

Mental Illness and Rational Decision Making

The mere correlation of suicide with mental illness or neurobiological changes does not prove that it cannot be voluntary or even rational. . . . A schizophrenic might decide that it is better to be dead than to remain schizophrenic; here the mental illness has the same role in a rational deliberation about suicide as any physical illness that is judged to be similarly unbearable and incurable. The same could even apply to depression: A depressed person who thought, on the basis of the evidence, that she would always be depressed might voluntarily and deliberately choose death over life. . . . One may be ill or abnormal, physically or mentally, and still be capable of real moral choice.

Margaret Pabst Battin, *Ethical Issues in Suicide*, 1995.

There is another way in which several contemporary authors have advocated universal, though not simultaneous, suicide: This is by recommending that the normal end of human life be voluntary death. According to this view, . . . most lives—except those snuffed out prematurely by accident or disease—would end, after reaching a normal lifespan, according to one's own plan at a time of one's own choosing, whether by means directly administered by oneself, or in voluntary euthanasia administered by a friend or physician. Suicide, in the form of a rationally planned death at a mature age, would become the usual and chosen way of dying; as medical prophylaxis and accident prevention improved, other deaths would decrease in relative frequency, and suicide would become indeed nearly universal. The question, "What if everybody did it?" should be answered, according to these authors, with a resounding "good!". . . .

Another type of antisuicide view assumes that suicide is wrong because it causes additional suicides, though there is an evident circularity in this reasoning. It is true that suicide rates do rise after the suicide of a public figure; that suicide rates are higher among children of persons who have killed themselves and in families where suicide has occurred; and that mimetic suicides frequently occur in which one individual replicates as precisely as possible the manner of someone else's suicide. Even suicides of fashion occur; the prototypes are the epidemic suicides among the maidens of Miletus (ended only by an edict that the bodies of the girls who had hanged themselves be carried naked through the marketplace), and the suicides of 804 males and 140 females who imitated a Japanese student's jump to her death in the Mihara-yama volcano in 1933. But the fact that one suicide is the occasion for or causes another does not in itself show that either is wrong; suicide must be shown to be wrong on other, independent grounds, before the fact that it may be the cause of additional suicides will count against it. The Greek and Roman Stoics thought of the noble suicides—Cato, Socrates, and Lucretia, for instance—as *examples* to be imitated by those with sufficient courage and strength to do so. David Hume, centuries later, said:

> If suicide be supposed a crime it is only cowardice can impel us to it. If it be no crime, both prudence and courage should engage us to rid ourselves at once of existence when it becomes a burden. It is the only way that we can be useful to society—by setting an example which, if imitated, would preserve to everyone his chance for happiness in life and would effectually free him from all danger of misery.

In considering the various major social arguments against suicide—that it hurts one's family, deprives society of an individual's labor or contribution, . . . we find that none of them independently serves as an adequate basis for a general argument against suicide.

> *"Almost no society has ever positively* encouraged *suicide, a few have* grudgingly tolerated it, *and most have* strenuously sought to limit it. *"*

Suicide Harms Society

Robert L. Barry

In the following viewpoint, Robert L. Barry, a Dominican priest and professor of religious studies at the University of Illinois, responds to Margaret Pabst Battin's argument that suicide does not necessarily harm society. Barry argues that self-killing does in fact cause severe harm to society since an individual's suicide inflicts severe grief on others, deprives the community of the individual's talents, and tempts others to take their own lives. For these reasons, writes Barry, the best policy is to prohibit or at least actively discourage suicide. Barry is the author of *Breaking the Thread of Life: On Rational Suicide*, from which this viewpoint is excerpted.

As you read, consider the following questions:

1. In Barry's opinion, how are teenage suicides especially harmful to the community?
2. In Barry's view, how have suicide advocates misconstrued the notion of basic human goodness?
3. What are the author's three objections to the argument that suicide should be permitted for individuals who cannot contribute to society?

W hat ultimately breaks the back of arguments for "socially beneficial" suicides is the near-impossibility of stopping irrational suicides that imitate "rational" or "beneficial" suicides. Allowing "socially beneficial suicides" would increase irrational suicides because they would make it easier for the irrational to justify their own self-killing. Even though curbing irrational suicide is difficult and radical measures have often been taken by societies to stop it, advocates of social suicide persist in believing it can be controlled. They ignore the fact that it is quite easy for societies to destroy themselves, and many societies that have adopted liberal suicide policies have vanished from history, while those such as the Moslem, Catholic, and Jewish communities have rejected these policies and have survived for hundreds of years.

If one were to take each of the social arguments against suicide individually, they might not appear that persuasive, but when considered together they argue rather powerfully that suicide for social reasons is extremely dangerous and should not be allowed. Permitting suicide for some members of society would create very sharp social divisions and would aggravate class divisions, for societies would be divided into those for whom it is permitted and those for whom it is prohibited. It is probably for this reason that almost no society has ever positively *encouraged* suicide, a few have grudgingly tolerated it, and most have strenuously sought to limit it.

The Harm Suicide Does to Society

Margaret Battin claims that arguments against social suicide are not solid, and she therefore concludes that suicide should be permitted. But it is not wise to discount these arguments, for they do raise some telling points against a liberal suicide policy. Here I wish to reiterate and evaluate some of the traditional arguments that have been made against suicide for social reasons to suggest that they retain their force and validity.

The first argument she rejects as insufficient holds that suicide can have ruinous psychological effects on families, causing long-term profound grief and severe guilt. Advocates of suicide argue that grief after suicide is not found in all societies, but only in those where suicide is viewed as wrong and immoral, which should make suicide permissible in some cases. Where suicides do no harm to families or friends, these advocates argue that there is no reason for prohibiting it. But contrary to their views, numerous studies have been done on suicide's impact on children and spouses, and the weight of evidence shows that it inflicts much harm, grief, and misery on survivors. The popular author Kurt Vonnegut reinforced this very simply: "Sons of suicide seldom do well." If there are families unharmed by suicide, they are not great enough in number to warrant a liberal policy.

But there is little to support the claim that suicide does not cause much grief and guilt in others, even where societies tolerate it. In spite of the fact that some forms of suicide were tolerated in Japan and India, survivors there still experienced much grief and guilt. While a few might welcome some suicides, most suffer from much grief despite their praise for a noble or honorable self-execution. Even the suicides of Seneca, Cato, Antony, Lucretia, and Socrates caused much grief to their friends, families, and associates, and these survivors would probably say that their grief, guilt, and loss far outweighed any social benefits that might have accrued from the suicides. There are few instances of suicide not causing grief among survivors, and when there is little grief it is because the suiciding person has acted so atrociously that survivors cannot grieve.

Suicide Destroys Human Bonds

Some of the oldest arguments against suicide claimed that it deprived society of needed gifts, talents, and contributions. Beccaria asserted that one who suicided harmed his nation by abandoning it, even though this was not the greatest evil one could do to one's community. St. Thomas Aquinas also held that suicide was harmful to society because

> every part belongs to the whole in virtue of what it is. But every man is part of the community, so that he belongs to the community in virtue of what he is. Suicide therefore involves damaging the community, as Aristotle makes clear.

There is much truth in this view and the harm suicide does to society is best seen in teenage suicide, for in these self-killings, the future talents, gifts, strength, and hope of the community are destroyed. Others have rejected this, but their rejection implies that the suicides of some socially "useless" people should be permitted because they make no significant contribution to society. John Donne, for example, argued that monks and hermits are not condemned for fleeing the state, which implies that suicides should be allowed for the socially useless. This rejection, however, not only has eugenic overtones, but also it is only tolerable if one considers societal contributions in the most narrow and materialistic terms possible. Permitting the unproductive (however they are classified) to self-execute would increase societal competition and interclass hatred and violence. This perspective on suicide would make a rather inhospitable environment for social critics whose contribution might be more negative than positive in many respects.

Suicide and Mental Illness

Research has shown that 90 percent of people who kill themselves have depression or another diagnosable mental or substance abuse disorder. In addition, research has shown that alterations in neurotransmitters such as serotonin are associated with the risk for suicide. Diminished levels have been found in patients with depression, impulsive disorders, a history of violent suicide attempts, and also in postmortem brains of suicide victims.

National Institute of Mental Health, *In Harm's Way: Suicide in America*, 1999.

Rejecting this criticism is unjustified because of its radically constricted notion of what constitutes the human good and because it presumes that the only real values in human life derive from individual acts and choices. It is closer to the truth to say that basic human goods derive not only from human choice, art, endeavor, and technology, but also from our very beings. The bonds between parents and children are not based solely on what they do with or to one another, but also on what they *are* to each other. Many family members who mourn suicides grieve because of what those who have suicided have *been* to them and not just because of what they did *for* them. To justify suicide for those who fail to meet criteria for being beneficial to society is contrary to much twentieth-century liberal ethos that has criticized its superficiality.

The Danger of Widespread Self-Killing

John Donne rightly noted that legalization of suicide would bring down the social and moral barriers against most forms of suicide and would result in widespread self-killing:

> [Y]et the number of wretched men on earth exceeds the happy (for every laborer is miserable and beastlike, in respect of the idle, abounding men). It was therefore thought necessary, by laws and opinion of religion . . . to take from these weary and macerated wretches their ordinary and open escape and ease, voluntary death.

Suicide proponents frequently dismiss arguments that legalizing suicide would induce others to suicide, but it is true that opening the door to suicide does lead others to consider it. Margaret Battin, for example, believes that even widespread suicide would not necessarily be a great harm to society. This is not what many people feel who consider themselves threatened by suicide. Legalizing suicide would create a culture in which self-killing would become commonplace, as recent trends show. Suicide is becoming more popular among AIDS patients, and their suicide rate is now sixty-six times the national average. The threat of widespread suicide is seen most clearly in the waves of suicides that have . . . swept communities of Native Americans. At the Warm Springs Reservation one percent of the tribe attempted suicide between January and March 1988, which is an annual suicide rate of four percent. Nationwide, young Indian men are killing themselves at a rate that is twice that of the national average for their age group. At the Wind River Reservation in central Wyoming, there were nine suicide attempts in five weeks. At the Alakanuk Reservation in Alaska, which has a population of only 550 people, eight Eskimos killed themselves. Suicide waves begin when an atmosphere of despair develops in a community that is difficult or impossible to abolish. When people feel themselves to be condemned and rejected by society, they kill themselves in reaction to it. This atmosphere of despair sweeps away the voiceless, despairing, weak, and troubled in our society and it is a real threat to them. Ray Calica of the Warm Springs Reservation summed it up perfectly when he said that "within the reservation some of these kids feel like fourth-rate citizens. They're told, 'Your ancestor was no good, and you're no good either.'"

Some suicide advocates argue that society has no obligation to protect those who are not able to reciprocate on account of physical or psychological impairments. Communities exist because individuals are selflessly willing to act for the good of others, and to allow some to destroy themselves because they cannot reciprocate eviscerates community. Endorsement of a liberal suicide policy shows how thinly some people view community and how willing they are to allow people to be destroyed to protect pure contentless individual autonomy.

Suicide for the Infirm or Disabled

Charlotte Gilman made the argument that people should not kill themselves when they still have an opportunity to do good or to perform morally good acts. But, in her later years, she was diagnosed with cancer and decided to commit suicide. She justified her suicidal wishes at that time by claiming that she could no longer do much good for anyone. This might sound like a justifiable reason for suiciding, but a closer analysis reveals its flaws. First, no matter how dismal a person's future might appear, one cannot say that no good can come from their being alive. Second, even if one is utterly incapable of actually doing good to others, one may still be able to do good to oneself. Helen Keller was able to do little good for herself or directly for others, but in response to her needs and very existence, great good came about. Third, one should not equate an inability to do good with doing evil, for small children cannot do much good, but that does not mean that they should self-execute.

A classical argument against suicide for the disabled has been that allowing this would brutalize the population at large. Against this traditional argument, Margaret Battin wonders if society can force these people to continue living:

> But to claim that those persons have an *obligation* to live (and suffer) in order to make normal individuals more humane or courageous is ethically questionable at best. One might also see it as a barbaric holdover of earlier European practices, according to which caged lunatics were placed on public display, criminals put in public stocks, and physically anomalous

The Common Law Tradition on Suicide

The common law tradition has held that the state has a clear interest in protecting innocent life and preventing its deliberate destruction, irrespective of any religious beliefs that might be involved. Besides seeking to preserve innocent human life from deliberate attack of any kind, the state has an interest in preserving the integrity of families and protecting children, the incompetent, disabled, and handicapped, and preserving the gifts and talents of the community. All of these interests bolster the state's concern for preventing suicide. The law has many interests to protect, and its barriers against suicide facilitate promoting this. The common law tradition has imposed different levels of punishment on suicidal acts at different times in history, not because it has considered suicide right at some times and wrong at others, but rather because in some times and places stronger punishments and measures were required to show the seriousness of suicide. These also indicate that at some times, societies were more blind to its evils than they were at others. It has often been the case that when societies did not penalize suicide, it was because it was not widely practiced and there was little need for laws against it. But when suicides became more common, penalties were imposed to strengthen preventative programs. Some societies have adopted a rather cavalier attitude toward suicide, but almost inevitably, these policies had to be reversed because suicides rose to an intolerable level.

Robert L. Barry, *Breaking the Thread of Life: On Rational Suicide*, 1994.

persons were displayed in circuses, presumably for the moral edification as well as entertainment of individuals not so afflicted.

She rightly argues that it is cruel and inhumane to subject the insane to mockery and ridicule, but she does not defeat the argument that allowing their suicides brutalizes others. This principle allows the insane to suicide, abandons them in their plight and brutalizes all in society. To legally permit the disabled to suicide is unfair to them and it would not build bonds of unity between the able-bodied and disabled. Arguing that the disabled who cannot reciprocate the good done for them should be allowed to suicide bites back because it would logically commit one to allowing the ungrateful to suicide. . . .

Suicide proponents approach this issue with a naively

confident spirit that there would be no harmful side effects from its legalization, that few people will be harmed, that it can be readily controlled, and that no one who does not wish to commit suicide will be brought to death. The arguments of suicide proponents that it should be permitted because of its benefit to society are unpersuasive because they do not grasp the serious threat that the harmful effects of suicide can pose to families, to the immature, to the emotionally and mentally unstable, or to society at large.

Periodical Bibliography

The following articles have been selected to supplement the diverse views presented in this chapter. Addresses are provided for periodicals not indexed in the *Readers' Guide to Periodical Literature*, the *Alternative Press Index*, the *Social Sciences Index*, or the *Index to Legal Periodicals and Books*.

Robert L. Barry	"The Biblical Teachings on Suicide," *Issues in Law & Medicine*, Winter 1997.
Robert P. George and William C. Porth Jr.	"Death, Be Not Proud," *National Review*, June 26, 1995.
John Hardwig	"Is There a Duty to Die?" *Hastings Center Report*, March/April 1997.
Gene Kasmar	"Suicide, an Ethical and Moral Alternative," *Human Quest*, May/June 1997. Available from 4300 NW 23rd Ave., Box 203, Gainesville, FL 32614-7050.
Bill Murchison	"The Dark, Dark Wood of Suicide," *Chronicles*, August 1998. Available from the Rockford Institute, 928 N. Main St., Rockford, IL 61103-7061.
David Novak	"Suicide Is Not a Private Choice," *First Things*, August/September 1997.
Julian Savulescu	"The Trouble with Do-Gooders: The Example of Suicide," *Journal of Medical Ethics*, April 1997. Available from BMJ Publishing Group, PO Box 590A, Kennebunkport, ME 04046.
Thomas Szasz	"Suicide as a Moral Issue," *Freeman*, July 1999.
Ernest van den Haag	"Make Mine Hemlock," *National Review*, June 12, 1995.
Brian Young	"Is Death a Constitutional Right? The Sanctity of Life," *World & I*, April 1994.
Wendy Murray Zoba	"The Way We Die," *Christianity Today*, April 8, 1996.

Should Society Condone Physician-Assisted Suicide?

Chapter Preface

The right-to-die movement is often identified with euthanasia—the act of killing or permitting the death of hopelessly sick or injured individuals in a relatively painless way for reasons of mercy. In "passive" euthanasia patients are allowed to die, as in the case of removing life support from a comatose patient. Passive euthanasia is accepted medical practice in the United States, and patients may sign "living wills" indicating that they do not wish to be kept alive by artificial means. "Active" euthanasia, on the other hand, is illegal in all parts of the world. It is defined as the actual killing of a patient, often by means of lethal injection.

Modern right-to-die advocates are more likely to support physician-assisted suicide than active euthanasia, and they are careful to distinguish between the two. In physician-assisted suicide (PAS), a doctor provides a patient with the means to end his or her life, for example, by allowing patients access to a lethal drug. Advocates believe that PAS gives patients total control over the dying process, allowing them to choose if and when to end their lives. Opponents of PAS believe it is little different than active euthanasia, since both involve one person helping another to die.

In 1998, the difference between assisted suicide and active euthanasia was dramatically demonstrated by Jack Kevorkian, a retired pathologist who claims to have helped over 130 people commit suicide since 1990. However, on November 23, 1998, *60 Minutes* aired a videotape of Kevorkian performing active euthanasia for the first time, as he injected Thomas Youk, a fifty-two-year-old Michigan native who suffered from Lou Gehrig's disease, with lethal medication.

The shocking display prompted quick action from Michigan authorities: Kevorkian was arrested and tried for murder. Unlike Kevorkian's previous trials, in this case the judge did not allow the defense to present testimony about Youk's pain and suffering, and emphasized that whether the victim consents is legally irrelevant in murder cases. A jury found Kevorkian guilty of second-degree murder, and on April 13, 1999, he was sentenced to ten to twenty-five years in prison.

The Kevorkian trial is evidence that many Americans

strongly object to active euthanasia. Opinions about assisted suicide, however, are more divided. Oregon legalized PAS for the terminally ill in 1994 (the law went into effect in 1997), and other states are considering doing the same. In the following chapter, authors debate whether physicians and individuals should support assisted suicide.

"Entailed in [the] right to live one's life is the freedom to choose to end it when, in one's judgment, it is no longer worth living."

Individuals Have a Right to Die

Andrew Bernstein

In the following viewpoint, philosophy professor Andrew Bernstein argues that Jack Kevorkian was fighting for individuals' right to die when he granted a terminally ill patient's request for euthanasia in November 1998. The right to die is an essential part of the freedom to control one's own life, the author maintains, and therefore laws prohibiting euthanasia and physician-assisted suicide are unjust. Bernstein is a senior writer for the Ayn Rand Institute, which promotes individual rights and limited government.

Editor's Note: The following viewpoint was written in March 1999, just as Kevorkian's trial was beginning; the suicide doctor was ultimately convicted of second-degree murder and sentenced to ten to twenty-five years in prison.

As you read, consider the following questions:
1. How many times has Kevorkian been acquitted of assisting in suicide, according to the author?
2. How does Bernstein answer the question "To whom does one's life belong?"
3. With what famous trial does the author compare the Kevorkian murder trial?

Excerpted from "'Dr. Death' Is a Defender of Life," by Andrew Bernstein, Ayn Rand Institute, found at www.aynrand.org/medialink/drdeath.shtml. Reprinted by permission.

D r. Jack Kevorkian's murder trial now beginning in Pontiac, Michigan involves far more than an individual's right to die: it involves his right to live.

Kevorkian, who has been acquitted in three previous assisted-suicide trials, is charged with first-degree murder for administering a lethal injection to a Michigan man who was dying of Lou Gehrig's disease. Kevorkian has openly stated his intent to make this a clear-cut test case for euthanasia.

But far more than euthanasia is going to be on trial. For if a man suffering from an agonizing terminal illness does not have the legal right to choose death—if the state can stop him and prolong his agony—then the question must be asked: to whom does one's life belong?

The Freedom to Choose

Surely, in a free country, the only moral answer is that a man's life belongs to himself. It is not the property of society or of the government. Each individual has the right to his own "life, liberty and the pursuit of happiness." Entailed in this right to live one's life is the freedom to choose to end it when, in one's judgment, it is no longer worth living. Just as the right to free speech includes the right to remain silent—just as the right to practice religion includes the right to be an atheist—so the right to live includes the right to decide to die. Freedom means the freedom to choose.

Clearly, choosing death is a serious matter, not to be done on the spur of the moment. But if, after serious reflection, a rational adult concludes that he prefers death, he must have the right to implement that decision. Consequently, he must have the right to request assistance from others; and, for the same reason, those others must have the right to provide whatever assistance is asked for.

The opponents of medically assisted suicide are plainly arguing from an anti-freedom premise. They are opposed to a man's right to live and to die by his own decision. "Consent is not a viable defense in taking the life of another," states the Michigan prosecutor who will try the case. But if my consent is not sufficient justification to terminate my life, what does this say regarding my freedom and my right to my own life? It says that I am a rightless pawn whom a paternalistic state can compel to suffer as it deems fit. It says that the most fundamental decision about the disposition of my life is to be made by others, against my will.

The Ultimate Civil Right

Our lives belong to us alone. With a large segment of the population—many of whom have witnessed the bad death of a parent—facing imminent death, the voice for a better death grows louder and more persistent. Assisted death for the mentally competent terminally ill adult who voluntarily requests it is the ultimate civil right, not unlike other minority rights fought for during [the 1960s]. As one California court put it, echoing the beliefs of the national majority: "The right to die is an integral part of our right to control our own destinies so long as the rights of others are not affected."

Derek Humphry and Mary Clement, *Freedom to Die*, 1998.

The issue of the right to control one's own body, free of government coercion, is not distinctive to euthanasia. It is the essence of political liberty—so that far more than the fate of Kevorkian or the status of assisted-suicide hinges on this upcoming trial.

Anti-Euthanasia Laws Are Unjust

Although Kevorkian may have broken the law, we must remember that so did Thomas Jefferson and the Founding Fathers—so did all those who, in pursuit of justice, sought to challenge the morality of the existing legal system. Kevorkian's courage in creating this test case is reminiscent of the Scopes "monkey trial" in 1925 in Dayton, Tennessee. When the Christian Fundamentalists, who controlled Tennessee's state legislature, passed a law prohibiting the teaching of evolution, John T. Scopes, a high school biology teacher, continued to teach Darwinian theory. He deliberately broke the law, initiating the "trial of the century" that resulted eventually in the repeal of the law.

The issues in Kevorkian's case are similar—as are his opponents. It is no accident that the strongest hostility toward euthanasia comes from devout religionists. For in their view, a man's life does not belong to himself, but to God.

The anti-evolution law did not permit a man to choose how to think; the anti euthanasia law does not permit a man to choose how to live. The first was directed against man's mind, the second against his body, but the principle is identical: the individual's life is ultimately to be controlled by some higher authority.

In the Scopes trial seventy-three years ago, the target of the prosecution was not simply a Tennessee schoolteacher, but the principle of the individual's right to think. Today, the spiritual heirs of those prosecutors will be placing on trial, not just Jack Kevorkian, but the individual's right to die— and hence right to live—as a free man.

"Physician-assisted suicide is presented as a private affair between two consenting adults. . . . But the taking of life is never simply a private affair."

Individuals Do Not Have a Right to Die

Peter J. Bernardi

Peter J. Bernardi, an assistant professor of religious studies at Loyola University in New Orleans, argues in the following viewpoint that individuals do not have a right to assisted suicide. Bernardi maintains that personal freedom must be balanced against individuals' responsibilities to the communities they live in: In his view, a right to suicide would be contrary to each person's responsibility to uphold the value of life. Bernardi believes that advocates of assisted suicide have failed to consider how acceptance of the practice would harm both terminally ill patients and society as a whole, and this has led them to falsely conclude that individuals have a right to die.

As you read, consider the following questions:
1. What does Bernardi say are the hallmarks of a just society?
2. In the author's view, what fundamental values have been "crowded out" by radical individualism?
3. What example does the author give to illustrate how the right to die could become a duty to die?

Excerpted from "Is Death a Right?" by Peter J. Bernardi, *Christianity Today*, May 20, 1996. Reprinted with permission from the author.

[A] hidden engine that drives the assisted-suicide cause is embedded in the ambiguous expressions "right to choose" and "right to die." This latter slogan first won currency in the legal debate over the patient's right to refuse unwanted treatment. But now the assisted-suicide movement uses "right to die" language to include active measures to terminate life. Underlying these catch phrases is the assumption that the individual's self-determination is sovereign, severed from the realities of truth and responsibility.

Valuing the worth of the individual is a supreme achievement of Western culture influenced by the Greek philosophical and Judeo-Christian traditions. The human person, created in God's image, has an incomparable dignity that gives rise to rights and responsibilities. Safeguarding these rights and promoting corresponding responsibilities are the hall-marks of a just society.

Individual Freedom vs. Public Morality and Social Order

However, as Mary Ann Glendon, professor of law at Harvard, has pointed out in *Rights Talk*, a hyper-rights rhetoric has taken hold in our society, leading to a radical individualism crowding out other fundamental values: that humans are essentially social, and that as individuals we have responsibilities to others. American rights rhetoric renders "extraordinary homage to independence and self-sufficiency, based on an image of the rights-bearer as a self-determining, unencumbered individual, a being connected to others only by choice." Our rights-talk recognizes the immediate and "personal dimensions of a problem, while it regularly neglects the moral, the long-term, and the social implications."

The ideal of total self-sufficiency, a radical version of individual autonomy, has become normative. Dependency is implicitly viewed as something to be avoided in oneself and disdained in others. Professor Glendon remarks: "By exalting autonomy to the degree we do, we systematically slight the very young, the severely ill or disabled, the frail elderly, as well as those who care for them."

The modern tradition of natural rights has repudiated the idea of the human person as "naturally" situated within and constituted through relationships of care and dependency. John Stuart Mill extended the domain of individual sovereignty, and he did so by virtue of a right: "the independence of the individual is, of right, absolute." Mill considered that interference with individual freedom was justified only to prevent harm to others. This principle has had a major impact on American jurisprudence, evolving into the right to privacy that served as the basis for *Roe v. Wade*. It also powers the suicide-rights movement.

The Inalienable Right to Life

In the America I know and love, there are inalienable rights. The cause for assisted suicide would not have gotten as far as it has if we paid more than lip service to our founding document and remembered the meaning and import of its words. The Declaration of Independence recognizes that there is a right to life and that it is an inalienable one, meaning it is a right that a person can never give up. It is not a right dependent on the largesse of the government or the people. It is not a right dependent on an individual's mental competence or willingness to give it up. It is inalienable.

The law does not recognize consent of a victim as a defense to a charge of murder any more than it recognizes consent to slavery. It doesn't matter how benign the slaveowner would be; it is a matter of principle, a matter of inalienable human rights.

And government's duty is to preserve and protect this right to life, enhance it, forbid any attempt by any one—private individual, doctor, even a state legislature—from attempting to recognize its alienation in any time, place, or manner by any one of its citizens.

So, there is no right of privacy that encompasses a right to suicide or assisted suicide. On the contrary, there is a right to life that is inalienable.

James M. Thunder, *Vital Speeches of the Day*, May 1, 1997.

This notion of the isolated, self-sufficient individual endowed with the right to privacy is a fiction. The radical rights rhetoric promotes an ethical relativism that destroys the common bonds necessary for maintaining human dignity and social order. Human beings are not isolated monads. We urgently need to retrieve in our rights discourse a sense of the person situated within, and partially constituted by, relationship with others. The movement to legalize assisted suicide plays on the pernicious separation between private and public morality that corrodes our society. Physician-assisted suicide is presented as a private affair between two consenting adults. Proponents thus artificially isolate assisted suicide from the social context in which physician and patient operate. But the taking of life is never simply a private affair.

The Right to Die May Become the Duty to Die

Radical autonomy is a deadly deception. Proponents of mercy killing argue for the right of mentally competent, terminally ill adults to receive a physician's assistance to commit suicide. The reality is that such autonomous requests will be subtly or not so subtly influenced by others.

A telling example of how easily the right to die can change into the duty to die appeared in a letter published in the Santa Rosa (California) *Press Democrat* from an 84-year-old woman who had been living with her daughter for 20 years. "Everything went fine for many years," the woman wrote, "but when I started to lose my hearing about three years ago, it irritated my daughter. . . . She began to question me about my financial matters and apparently feels I won't leave much of an estate for her. . . . She became very rude to me. . . . Then suddenly, one evening, my daughter said very cautiously she thought it was o.k. for older people to commit suicide if they cannot take care of themselves." After recounting the ways her daughter reinforced this message, the woman commented: "So here I sit, day after day, knowing what I am expected to do when I need a little help."

"Why not allow physicians to secretly provide patients with drugs enabling suicidal patients to kill themselves?"

Physicians Should Grant Requests for Assistance in Suicide

Joram Graf Haber

In the following viewpoint, Joram Graf Haber, a professor of philosophy at New Jersey's Bergen Community College, contends that when a patient's decision to commit suicide is rational, there are no ethical reasons for physicians to refuse the request for assisted suicide. However, Haber does not believe that physician-assisted suicide (PAS) should be legalized, since in his view that could lead to very ill patients feeling obligated to choose PAS or doctors becoming too quick to recommend the option. Instead, he contends that PAS should be tolerated as a "poorly kept secret": Assisted suicide should not be officially condoned, but neither should doctors who grant requests for PAS be prosecuted as criminals.

As you read, consider the following questions:

1. What is the difference between assisted suicide and active euthanasia, in the author's opinion?
2. What subspecialty of medicine has Jack Kevorkian proposed?
3. What other policies does Haber cite as examples of "poorly kept secrets"?

Excerpted from "Should Physicians Assist the Reaper?" by Joram Graf Haber, *Cambridge Quarterly of Healthcare Ethics*, Winter 1996. Reprinted with permission from the Cambridge University Press.

Physician-assisted suicide is a novel idea having affinities with both suicide and euthanasia. It has affinities with suicide because it involves a self-inflicted death, and it has affinities with euthanasia because the physician is instrumental in the death. It is, however, not exactly either, making it the subject of an exciting debate.

Those who oppose physician-assisted suicide do so: (1) because it is *suicide* and they are opposed to *suicide*; (2) because it is *assisted* and they are opposed to *assisting* suicide; or (3) because it is *physician-assisted* and they are opposed to *physicians* assisting suicide. In the following I will discuss each of these objections and see what they have to recommend them. Not surprisingly, while (3) includes the strongest objection, it is not an objection that cannot be overcome.

Suicide Can Be Rational

Those who oppose physician-assisted suicide because it is *suicide* argue that suicide is irrational or, if it is rational, that it is immoral. Those who argue that it is irrational contend that anyone who would contemplate killing herself is invariably depressed and unable to assess the value of living. Caught in the throes of a debilitating depression, the argument is that one will imprudently assign greater weight to the costs of living than to the benefits thereof. Psychiatrists, in particular, are fond of this tack. They argue that, more often than not, one contemplating suicide could be helped if administered appropriate therapy.

While not denying the ability of a depression to cloud our judgment and undermine the value of living, the argument from depression proves too much. Not everyone who is depressed is incapable of balancing the costs against the benefits of living. People who are terminally ill, suffering, and have no reasonable chance of recovery, hardly underestimate the value of life. For them, the costs of living outweigh the benefits. A decision to stop living thus can hardly be labeled irrational. As Richard Brandt has put it, if between two future world courses, it is manifest that one of them is not preferable to eliminating one's present misery, then under conditions of optimal information, it is not irrational to seek an early demise.

Suicide Can Be Moral

Those who argue that suicide is immoral argue that life is a gift from God and it is for God to decide when it should end. The earliest expression of this view is found in *Phaedo*, where Plato has Socrates awaiting his executioner and ruminating about his impending death. Believing that upon death the soul is freed from the body to pursue unadulterated intellectual pursuits, Socrates remarks: "Show me a man who is a true philosopher and I'll show you a man who desires death." When asked by a disciple why he does not then kill himself, Socrates replies that his life belongs to the gods and is not his to take. The "divine ownership argument," as I shall call it, is echoed later in history by St. Thomas Aquinas who argues that suicide is a breach of God's sovereignty over us, and Immanuel Kant according to whom "God is our owner." The argument is also made by modern-day Catholics and Orthodox Jews.

Naturally, the divine ownership argument is persuasive only if one believes in God and then, too, only if one believes that God forbids suicide. Without this belief, the argument is unpersuasive. Of course, there may be nontheistic arguments against suicide such as the natural law argument that suicide violates the laws of nature or the Kantian argument that in killing ourselves we act on a principle that, if universalized, would contradict life itself. But none of these arguments is terribly convincing. We are left, then, with a cost-benefit analysis that argues for suicide in just those cases where the costs of living outweigh the benefits.

Is Assisting in Suicide the Same as Killing?

Those who oppose physician-assisted suicide because it is assisted argue that it is no different from euthanasia by which is meant *active euthanasia*. Active euthanasia, in contrast with *passive euthanasia*, refers to the killing of a person for reasons concerning mercy rather than malice. The typical scenario involves a patient who is terminally ill, suffering, and has no reasonable chance of recovery. Rather than let that person wallow in pain, a close relative of that person (or a friend) causes death in that person usually by administering a lethal dose of morphine. Passive euthanasia, by contrast, refers to the failure to take affirmative measures to extend a dying person's life. Usually, this involves withholding ordinary or extraordinary life support or executing a Do Not Resuscitate Order (DNR), but sometimes involves withholding food and water or turning off a respirator.

It is common for bioethicists to distinguish between active and passive euthanasia. Passive euthanasia is generally condoned because it is the patient's condition that causes death. Active euthanasia is generally condemned because the cause of death is another person, and killing a person is put forward as wrong. This is the position of the American Medical Association and the one traditionally found in common law. Historically, the law has not distinguished between murder and active euthanasia because it has never recognized motive as an element of a crime. All that is necessary for a murder to occur is that the agent intend to kill another person and that the agent act on that intent. The agent's motives for killing have never been relevant to whether a killing is a murderous one.

But assisted suicide is not euthanasia. As its name suggests, assisted suicide is where one individual, physician or not, provides another individual with the means to kill himself. Giving a gun to a dying patient so that the patient may kill himself, then, is an example of assisted suicide. Unlike active euthanasia where the agent of death is someone other than the patient, in assisted suicide the patient himself is the agent of death.

Still, if active euthanasia is wrong because it involves the active participation of another agent, so is assisting suicide wrong (the argument goes), because it too involves the agency of another. Otherwise put, to the extent that assisted suicide is more like euthanasia than it is like suicide, the agent of death is not unaccountable. What we need to ask, then, is even if assisted suicide is more like euthanasia than it is like suicide, is euthanasia morally wrong?

Killing Is Not Always Wrong

As alluded to earlier, critics of euthanasia oppose the practice because it involves killing a person, and that is something that we ought not to do. But it is not that killing a person is wrong *simpliciter*, it is wrong in the absence of a compelling reason. With the exception of pacifists, most people cite self-defense as such a reason, but friends of the death penalty cite retribution and deterrence as others. And even those who think the fetus is a person may favor abortion in certain situations. So, while life is sacred and ought to be treated with the utmost respect, this does not mean that we ought never to kill. What we ought never to do is kill in the absence of a compelling reason.

Is killing to alleviate suffering a compelling reason? That, of course, is the question at issue. And while reasonable people may disagree on this question, they must agree that the distinction between active and passive euthanasia cannot be made on the grounds that active euthanasia involves a killing and killing is something we ought never to do. We simply do not hold to any such principle. Then, if those who oppose physician-assisted suicide do so out of their opposition to it being an assisted killing, this by itself will be less than convincing.

Physicians Can Prevent Mistakes and Abuses

There remains the opposition to the *physician* being the one who is the agent of death. Dr. Jack Kevorkian, who has taken care to distinguish euthanasia from physician-assisted suicide, has argued that physicians should be the ones responsible for assisting patients with carrying out their suicidal wishes. As Kevorkian envisions, patients wishing to die would be provided with either a "suicide machine" that could be operated by pushing a lever with one finger to inject a lethal dose of potassium chloride through an intravenous needle, or with a mask through which they could breathe carbon monoxide. (Other proponents of physician-assisted suicide argue for allowing physicians to prescribe life-ending drugs.) By such means, patients otherwise unable to kill themselves could carry out their suicidal wishes and be the agents of their own deaths.

Kevorkian proposes that a subspecialty in medicine be formed, "obitiatry" (from the Latin and Greek roots for "doctor" and "death"), and that obitiatrists specialize in "medicide," Kevorkian's term for medically assisted suicide.

As he sees it, there is a grave danger in leaving the dilemma of assisting suicide to nonphysicians. For one thing, such a practice could lead to abuse caused by familial disputes and economic factors; for another, mistakes could be made based on faulty medical information. He cites the tragic case of a Californian woman whose son gave her a gun with which she killed herself after she was mistakenly diagnosed as having a brain tumor.

To help curb mistakes and abuses, Kevorkian proposes that a panel of five obitiatrists be required to participate in each death, actively or in a consulting capacity. Three of the five would serve in an advisory capacity to decide whether death is justifiable, with at least one of the three being a psychiatrist. For the death to take place, all three advisory obitiatrists would have to concur. Furthermore, the patient would have to review all evaluations on an ongoing basis. If the patient shows any semblance of ambivalence, the entire procedure would be stopped and the patient could no longer or ever again be a candidate for "medicide."

Objections to Physician-Assisted Suicide

Having evaluated the arguments against physician-assisted suicide due to its being both suicide and assisted, and having discussed Kevorkian's arguments in favor of the practice, what are the arguments against it? There are many. First, patients could wind up being pressured to kill themselves because of such considerations as the cost of health care. Second, doctors could recommend suicide for the wrong reasons such as unconscious biases against minorities, people with AIDS, or even a misdiagnosis of a terminal illness. Third, patients usually follow doctors' recommendations and if doctors were to suggest an easy death, seriously ill or poorly educated patients might not feel strong enough to make their own reasoned decisions. (Driving this argument is the fear of putting too much power into the hands of physicians.)

A fifth argument against physician-assisted suicide is that people prone to consider suicide might view it as an acceptable option before exhausting all treatment modalities. In other words, there is concern that legalizing physician-assisted suicide would make it too easy to not think of ways to help people live. Yet a sixth argument concerns the impact that a field like obitiatry might have on our perception of physicians as health care providers. The perception we have is that they are professionals committed to promoting health and extending life. This perception would change to our detriment if physicians were engaged in death-causing practices. And because perception is reality for many patients, our already stretched thin confidence in health care providers might be damaged well beyond repair.

Achieving a Good Death

When death is the only way to relieve suffering, and inevitable regardless, why not allow it to come in the most humane and dignified way possible? Why is it considered ethical to die of "natural causes" after a long heroic fight against illness filled with "unnatural" life-prolonging medical interventions, and unethical to allow patients to take charge at the end of a long illness and choose to die painlessly and quickly? Most of us hope to be fortunate enough to experience a "good death" when we have to die, and to be spared an agonizing ordeal at the very end. Many of us hope that if we do end up in such unfortunate circumstances, we can find a physician who will help us creatively explore all possibilities, including facilitating a relatively quick and painless death. Hopefully we will never need it, but the possibility would be very reassuring.

Timothy E. Quill, *Death and Dignity: Making Choices and Taking Charge*, 1994.

Finally, there are those who argue that legalizing physician-assisted suicide would erode the value of human life. Recalling the horrors of the Nazi holocaust that at first involved euthanasia, albeit of an involuntary nature, the fear here is that making any inroads on the sanctity of human life puts us on the thin edge of a dangerous wedge. That the dangers of this are real enough can be seen from those friends of physician-assisted suicide who argue that beyond those cases involving dying patients in agonizing pain, physician-assisted suicide should be extended to such incapacitating illnesses as crippling arthritis, emphysema, degenerative neurological diseases, and stroke. Kevorkian himself endorses medicide for such cases, although he stops short (for the moment) at depression and psychiatric illnesses.

Should physicians then "assist the Reaper?" If what I have said is correct, there are no conceptual reasons why they should not: suicide is not obviously wrong unless one is a theist, and with the exception of pacifists, assisted suicide is not obviously tantamount to murder. The objections to physician-assisted suicide are largely of a practical nature obtained when the practice is institutionalized.

Permitted but Not Explicitly Condoned

But what if it were not institutionalized but administered secretly, not unlike the way DNR orders were once administered? Before passive euthanasia became widely accepted, patients not wanting life-support treatment would typically convey their wishes to their treating physicians at which time the physicians would issue a DNR order, often on a blackboard that would later be erased. (They would carry out this order by failing to call a "code.") In this way, physicians would give effect to their patients' desires and at the same time avoid legal complications. Then why not allow physicians to secretly provide patients with drugs enabling suicidal patients to kill themselves? Doing so would at least have the virtue of sidestepping the practical problems associated with making medicide a subspecialty of medicine and legitimizing the field of obitiatry. Furthermore, because it matters to us how we die, receiving drugs "under the table" is a less chilling death than death by means of a macabre killing machine.

The problem with condoning noninstitutionalized physician-assisted suicide, however, is that it violates the publicity criterion of morality that forbids us to act in ways that we cannot advocate to be publicly allowed. In many views, a necessary feature of morality is that what it recommends and prohibits should be known and understood by those to whom it applies. In *Perpetual Peace*, for instance, Kant proposed as a "transcendental condition of public law" that "any actions affecting the rights of other people must be capable of full publicity; else they are unjust." It is this condition that explains why, for example, many of us object to the utilitarian claim that it is permissible to secretly lynch an innocent person in an effort to quench a blood-thirsty mob. But if morality forbids us to act in ways that we cannot publicly advocate be allowed, then it would presumably forbid the secretive practice of physician-assisted suicide.

A Poorly Kept Secret

But perhaps we could satisfy the publicity criterion if we distinguished between a strong and weak sense of the criterion and argue that it satisfies the weakened sense. I submit that there is such a weakened sense that is satisfied by the concept of a "poorly kept secret." Poorly kept secrets are secrets that are, in an attenuated sense, advocated as publicly allowed. As alluded to earlier, before it became official policy, it was a poorly kept secret that physicians would allow patients to die when they did not desire life-extending treatment. Today, it is a poorly kept secret that one can exceed 55 mph on most interstate highways without being ticketed, that there are gays in the military, and that there are professors who allow their students to improve their grades through extra-credit assignments.

Now the question we must ask is what have poorly kept secrets to recommend for them that publicly allowed practices do not? The answer I propose is that for certain practices, it is problematic to publicly advocate allowing them in a way that secretly allowing them is not, and disallowing them altogether is. Take the example of gays in the military and the Pentagon's policy (before it was ruled unconstitutional) of "don't ask, don't tell." Without commenting on the merits of the Pentagon's argument, it was thought that allowing gays to serve in the military by not revealing their sexual orientation was preferable to publicly allowing them to serve on the one hand and disallowing them to serve on the other. The argument was that to publicly advocate that they be allowed to serve would disrupt troop cohesiveness and morale, while publicly advocating that they not be allowed to serve was discriminatory. The alternative was to allow them to serve in secret—a secret everyone knew. Similarly, there may be very good reasons for not raising the speed limit as well as not enforcing the present one: to raise the speed limit might encourage motorists to exceed that limit making traveling even more precarious than it is. At the same time, 55 mph is slow given today's super highways and turbo-driven cars. And there may also be good reasons for Professor X's not trumpeting his extra-credit policy of allowing his students to improve their grades through extra-credit assignments. Besides the inconvenience of having to grade the plethora of papers submitted by those taking advantage of his policy, publicly advocating his policy might be tantamount to giving his students a distinct assignment undercutting its value as "extra" credit. At the same time, there are good reasons for providing students with extra opportunities to improve their grades.

Not a Perfect Solution, but a First Step

In conclusion, I have argued that while physician-assisted suicide is not problematic as a conceptual matter, there are practical objections to advocating that it be publicly allowed, but that these objections can be cured if the practice is tolerated as a poorly kept secret. To be sure, keeping physician-assisted suicide a poorly kept secret is not a panacea. For one thing, keeping physician-assisted suicide a secret makes it a practice that is difficult to assess. How, we might ask, are we to reconcile the practice with physician accountability and patients' rights? For another thing, it presupposes that physicians and patients could informally agree on a best course of action. Furthermore, we would at some point want to bring the poorly kept secret in line with such related concepts as condonation and self-deception and want to know how our endorsing a poorly kept secret relates to such fundamental values as honesty, truthfulness, and integrity. But whatever analysis remains to be done, the concept has the virtue of enabling us to meet what I perceive to be the greatest objections to publicly advocated physician-assisted suicide, and goes some way to quelling whatever ambivalence we might have about a practice that is emotionally charged but nonetheless inviting.

| *"Life's value dictates that one person should not facilely be allowed to participate in deciding the fate of another."*

Physicians Should Not Grant Requests for Assistance in Suicide

R. Henry Capps Jr.

In the viewpoint that follows, R. Henry Capps Jr. states that physicians have a moral duty to respect their patient's wishes. However, he argues, because most suicidal patients suffer from depression, physicians must question the rationality of patients who say they want to die. Furthermore, writes Capps, many patients' requests for assisted suicide stem from the pain associated with terminal illness, which he contends can be relieved through palliative care. For these reasons, the author believes that physicians should always seek alternatives to helping their patients commit suicide. At the time this viewpoint was originally published, Capps was studying for a career as a family physician at East Carolina University School of Medicine.

As you read, consider the following questions:

1. How does the World Health Organization define palliative care, as paraphrased by the author?
2. According to the author, why is suicide not a true expression of patient autonomy?
3. In Capps's view, why have physicians traditionally been fearful of using adequate pain-control medication?

Excerpted from "Physician-Assisted Suicide or Palliative Care? The Role of Physicians in Caring for Aged and Dying Patients," by R. Henry Capps Jr., *National Forum: The Phi Kappa Phi Journal*, vol. 78, no. 2, Spring 1998. Copyright ©1998 by R. Henry Capps. Reprinted with permission from the publishers.

I will prescribe regimen for the good of my patients according to my ability and judgment and never do harm to anyone. To please no one will I prescribe a deadly drug, nor give advice which may cause his death. . . . But I will preserve the purity of my life and my art.

—Excerpt from Hippocratic Oath

Physicians face many personal and ethical challenges in providing care for dying and aged patients. The development of new life-sustaining technology and an aging American population have produced a changing health care environment in relation to end-of-life choices. Once, physicians offered few life-sustaining medical treatments and limited comfort care. Death was sometimes cruel and painful. Today, life-prolonging and proposed life-ending treatments pose a challenge to the ethical assessment of proper end-of-life medical care. In times to come, the assessment of a dying patient may include two distinct methods and philosophies of providing for a less painful and less cruel death—physician-assisted suicide and palliative care. Proponents of the "right to die" have energized support for physician-assisted suicide, often overlooking significant technological advances in palliative care.

The Importance of Palliative Care

The World Health Organization defines palliative care as comprehensive medical care for patients whose disease has no other curative treatments. The same organization identifies components of palliative care as including symptom relief, pain relief, psychosocial therapy, and pastoral care. While palliative-care measures emphasize the quality of life of the individual and family, physician-assisted suicide addresses the eminent death of the patient by providing the mechanism for patients to end their life at a chosen time. The physician may or may not be present when the suicidal act occurs. Although debates have raged concerning the moral and ethical dilemmas posed by physician-assisted suicide, no acceptable resolution has arisen.

Physicians and society must be actively involved in shaping future medical standards of care for dying and aged patients, while employing a rigorous standard of ethics and morality. I believe that palliative care offers a more ethical therapy for a dying patient than physician-assisted suicide by enhancing patient autonomy, reducing suffering in the final days of life, and preserving the therapeutic role of the physician. The effective administration of palliative care should become the foundation for providing a more dignified and moral end-of-life therapy.

Suicide and Patient Autonomy

Physicians have a moral and professional duty to respect and encourage patient autonomy and self-determination. The application of this responsibility, however, sometimes becomes more challenging as a patient ages and sickens. Terminally ill patients may suffer cognitive, emotional, and psychological deficits that can undermine their capacity to exercise their autonomy. The approach a physician assumes with a dying patient should reflect this reality. Physicians must be especially scrupulous in considering the possibility of competency deficiencies in suicidal terminal patients.

Proponents of physician-assisted suicide might argue that a reasoned plea for help by suicide is competent based upon the patient's present or future quality of life. Proponents contend that a patient with autonomous desires, including suicide, should have those desires honored regardless of other ethical standards. The patient is reasoned to have a new understanding of death that allows competent decision-making in seeking a physician's guidance with suicide. Death is implied to be the only quality-of-life improvement option.

However, I believe that a patient's competence to make an autonomous decision *always* must be questioned if the patient wishes to commit suicide. Suicide is not a true expression of autonomy, because the nature of the suicidal act is both violent and hurtful. Patients with terminal illnesses certainly face terrible situations, but suicide is at best a questionably competent response. Three major criteria apply to the evaluation of the competency of any patient. The patient should "communicate and understand relevant information," "reason and deliberate about alternative treatments," and "possess goals and values by which to assess alternatives." A suicidal person may or may not fail the first two criteria of competence, but every suicidal person fails the third criterion.

The psychology of suicide prevents suicidal patients from properly appraising their goals and values. Most suicidal patients who succeed at killing themselves do so accidentally. Greater than 90 percent of suicidal patients (whether terminally ill or healthy) exhibit symptoms of depression or are suffering a psychiatric illness. Upon presentation to a physician, a suicidal patient who suffered from a psychiatric disorder or who was not terminally ill would immediately be hospitalized. The traditional standard of care for suicidal or psychiatric patients has included heroic measures such as hospitalization, regardless of their wishes. Suicidal patients who are not terminally ill are deemed incompetent to make the health care decisions based upon the third criteria of competency, despite apparent rationality. A terminally ill or dying patient should not be judged by a less rigorous standard of competency than a healthy individual. And certainly terminal illnesses do not provide a mystical understanding of death or suicide.

Proponents of physician-assisted suicide would argue that the only peaceful means of death is by suicide, when one can

Reprinted by permission of Chuck Asay and Creator's Syndicate.

determine the time and means of death. Proponents argue that a physician-assisted suicide is painless and simple. However, assisting a patient may be the easiest means of terminal health care, but it certainly is not the most ethical. Suicide by nature is neither painless nor simple, but very taxing spiritually and physically. Often patients who are committing suicide gasp for breath, struggle for continued life, or call for help. In the book *Final Exit*, Derek Humphry of the National Hemlock Society provides guidelines for suicidal acts. The National Hemlock Society recommends suffocation in addition to lethal medication for the commission of suicide. In addition, the physician (or suicide helper) must suppress the patient's attempts to remove the asphyxiate by physically restraining the arms and legs. Is this a peaceful death or a violent murder? While the methodology of assisted suicide would certainly be refined in a health care environment where physician-assisted suicide was accepted, the euphemistic refinement in the methodology would not change the violence of suicide or patients' last struggles for their lives. Suicide in any form is not a natural death.

Physicians' Duty to Do No Harm

The therapeutic role of the physician certainly is challenged by the dying patient. A physician's responsibility is to aid in the healing of patients, and death is seldom a desired outcome of a healing treatment. Traditionally, the therapeutic role of physicians has held to the philosophy of doing no harm. If a physician seeks to do no harm to his patients, how can the therapeutic role justify a physician's assistance in suicide? The technology to kill someone has been present for many years, but physician-assisted suicide is a modern issue. Why would helping to kill a patient seem more therapeutic today than thirty years ago?

Proponents of the "right to die" movement have argued that physicians should extend their therapeutic spectrum to include helping patients die. Proponents argue that the act of killing is far less harmful than the act of prolonging life by futile treatment. But when faced with a suicidal individual, a physician, like any other citizen, would be accountable for providing a lethal weapon such as a gun to the individual.

Patients who seek medication to end their lives pose a similar dilemma, only asking for a different type of lethal weapon. Is the physician any less accountable? Life's value dictates that one person should not facilely be allowed to participate in deciding the fate of another. Ending life in the face of viable palliative alternatives is clearly harmful. Physicians must do no harm to preserve the public's trust and their own therapeutic role.

Relieving Pain Through Palliative Care

One of the greatest fears of a dying patient is not death, but the pain associated with the final days of life. Physician attitudes toward dying patients must include compassion for physical and psychological pain. Technology has provided physicians with many new choices in controlling the pain and symptoms of patients. Most proponents and opponents of physician-assisted suicide consider pain relief a key issue in providing meaningful care to dying patients.

Unfortunately, physicians' training has lagged behind the new technologies and pain medicines. Physicians have traditionally been fearful of using adequate pain control out of fear of the addictive or other harmful properties of pain medications. Terminally ill patients are in special situations; clearly, pain control is far more important for them than a nebulous avoidance of potentially harmful properties of pain medication. The attitudes of physicians toward pain relief in the final days of a patient's life may significantly alter a patient's perspective on the possibility of physician-assisted suicide.

Palliative care provides a means to care for dying patients and their families. This philosophy of care provides for both psychological and physical pains. Palliative-care physicians are diligent in using proper medications such as opioids at indicated levels to maintain the patient's comfort. The physician must also address psychological and spiritual issues. A dying patient has many unique concerns and feelings. Dying patients face the psychological reconciliation of very painful losses, even painful enough to wish the hastening of death. The physician must bear in mind and understand each of these losses. The transition from life to death does not have to be violent but can be peaceful.

Guiding Patients to a Natural Death

Physician training also has neglected training physicians to deal with spiritual issues such as the realization of hope. Dying or aged patients who have a deteriorating quality of life and have lost all hope of improvement are more likely to request physician-assisted suicide. Physicians should be better trained to evaluate the needs of patients and counsel patients in understanding their disease, establishing adequate support systems, and reestablishing realistic hope. Physician-assisted suicide has garnered support in part because medical training is failing to prepare physicians for compassionate end-of-life care. The attitudes of future physicians must be redirected to caring compassionately for dying patients.

Palliative care offers an alternative to killing the patient that preserves the therapeutic role. The therapeutic role of providing a smooth, comfortable transition to death is more healing than aiding patients in ending their lives. The moral duty of physicians mandates the protection of life while respecting the feelings of the patient. Caring for a dying patient is demanding. Some technological medical treatments have extended the natural course of life and death. Especially as society becomes more elderly, the use of technology must not be abused either to hasten death or prolong life futilely. Instead, physicians have a moral responsibility to provide necessary care to aid patients in a painless progression to natural death.

The role of the physician in caring for the families of dying patients is also significant. Family members often have difficulty coping with the impending loss of their loved ones. The therapeutic role of the physician in caring for family members certainly is not addressed by physician-assisted suicide. Families must cope not only with the loss of their loved ones but also with the manner of death. The stigma of suicide often deepens grief, while the emotional support provided by a physician during palliative care may enable families in easing their grief and accepting the death. In a palliative-care setting, physicians can aid dying patients with the transition to death while assisting family members with the changes in life without special loved ones.

Physicians Must Oppose Assisted Suicide

Physicians' attitudes toward dying patients will shape the type of care a patient receives. Although the movement in society to encourage physician-assisted suicide probably will continue, physicians must play an active role in preserving patient autonomy, reducing pain, and fulfilling their professional mandates in the therapeutic role. These important components of caring for dying patients and their families can be fulfilled most clearly by effective palliative care. The physician's therapeutic role with a dying patient must be cherished, lest physicians and society forget the most fundamental tenets of medicine—to do no harm and to comfort ill and aged patients.

"The reason that polls in this country . . . show 60 to 80 percent support for legalization of assisted suicide is that people want to know they will have a way out if their suffering becomes too great."

Physician-Assisted Suicide Should Be Legalized

Faye Girsh

Faye Girsh is the executive director of the Hemlock Society, a national organization dedicated to the legalization of voluntary physician-assisted suicide (PAS) for terminally ill patients. In the viewpoint that follows, she contends that proposals to legalize PAS in various states enjoy much popular support, and that the examples of Oregon, the Netherlands, and Switzerland, where PAS is permitted, demonstrate that assisted suicide will not become widespread once it is legalized. In fact, she writes, legalizing PAS will help prevent abuse, since the practice will be strictly regulated. According to Girsh, most opposition to legalized PAS comes from the Catholic Church and other well-funded religious groups.

As you read, consider the following questions:

1. In Girsh's opinion, what causes people to ask for a hastened death?
2. According to the author, how many people took advantage of the Oregon Death with Dignity Act, which legalized physician-assisted suicide for terminally ill patients, in the first eight months the law was in effect?
3. What safeguards have been incorporated into the proposed death-with-dignity laws, as described by the author?

M any people agree that there are horrifying situations at the end of life which cry out for the help of a doctor to end the suffering by providing a peaceful, wished-for death. But, opponents argue, that does not mean that the practice should be legalized. They contend that these are the exceptional cases from which bad law would result.

I disagree. It is precisely these kinds of hard deaths that people fear and that happen to seven to ten percent of those who are dying that convince them to support the right to choose a hastened death with medical assistance. The reason that polls in this country—and in Canada, Australia, Great Britain and other parts of Europe—show 60 to 80 percent support for legalization of assisted suicide is that people want to know they will have a way out if their suffering becomes too great. They dread losing control not only of their bodies but of what will happen to them in the medical system. As a multiple-sclerosis patient wrote to the Hemlock Society: "I feel like I am just rotting away. . . . If there is something that gives life meaning and purpose it is this: a peaceful end to a good life before the last part of it becomes even more hellish."

Hospice Care Is Not Enough

Even with the best of hospice care people want to know that there can be some way to shorten a tortured dying process. A man whose wife was dying from cancer wrote, "For us, hospice care was our choice. We, however, still had 'our way,' also our choice, as 'our alternative.' We were prepared. And the 'choice' should be that of the patient and family."

It is not pain that causes people to ask for a hastened death but the indignities and suffering accompanying some terminal disorders such as cancer, stroke and AIDS. A survey in the Netherlands found that the primary reason to choose help in dying was to avoid "senseless suffering."

Hospice can make people more comfortable, can bring spiritual solace and can work with the family, but—as long as hospice is sworn neither to prolong nor hasten death—it will not be the whole answer for everyone. People should not have to make a choice between seeking hospice care and choosing to hasten the dying process. The best hospice care should be available to everyone, as should the option of a quick, gentle, certain death with loved ones around when the suffering has become unbearable. Both should be part of the continuum of care at the end of life.

We have the right to commit suicide and the right to refuse unwanted medical treatment, including food and water. But what we don't have—unless we live in Oregon—is the right to get help from a doctor to achieve a peaceful death. As the trial judge in the Florida case of *Kirscher vs McIver*, an AIDS patient who wanted his doctor's help in dying, said in his decision: "Physicians are permitted to assist their terminal patients by disconnecting life support or by prescribing medication to ease their starvation. Yet medications to produce a quick death, free of pain and protracted agony, are prohibited. This is a difference without distinction."

Very Few Patients Choose Assisted Suicide

The Oregon example has shown us that, although a large number of people want to know the choice is there, only a small number will take advantage of it. During the first eight months of the Oregon "Death with Dignity" law, only ten people took the opportunity to obtain the medications and eight used them to end their lives. In the Netherlands it consistently has been less than five percent of the total number of people who die every year who choose to get help in doing so from their doctor.

In Switzerland, where physician-assisted death also is legal, about 120 people die annually with the help of medical assistance. There is no deluge of people wanting to put themselves out of their misery nor of greedy doctors and hospitals encouraging that alternative. People want to live as long as possible. There are repeated testimonials to the fact that people can live longer and with less anguish once they know that help will be available if they want to end it. Even Jack Kevorkian, who says he helped 130 people die since 1990, has averaged only fourteen deaths a year.

To the credit of the right-to-die movement, end-of-life care has improved because of the push for assisted dying. In Oregon, end-of-life care is the best in the country: Oregon is No. 1 in morphine use, twice as many people there use hospice as the national average and more people die at home than in the hospital. In Maine there will be an initiative on the ballot in 2000 to legalize physician aid in dying, and in Arizona a physician-assisted-dying bill has been introduced. In both states the Robert Woods Johnson Foundation has awarded sizable grants to expand hospice care and to improve end-of-life care.

It is gratifying that the specter of assisted dying has spurred such concern for care at the end of life. Clearly, if we take the pressure off, the issue will disappear back into the closet. No matter how good the care gets, there still will be a need to have an assisted death as one choice. The better the care gets, the less that need will exist.

Answering Religious and "Slippery Slope" Objections to Assisted Suicide

The pope and his minions in the Catholic Church, as well as the religious right, announce that assisted dying is part of the "culture of death." Murder, lawlessness, suicide, the cheapening of life with killing in the media, the accessibility of guns, war—those create a culture of death, not providing help to a dying person who repeatedly requests an end to his or her suffering by a day or a week. Not all religious people believe that. The Reverend Bishop Spong of the Episcopal Diocese of Newark, New Jersey, said: "My personal creed asserts that every person is sacred. I see the holiness of life enhanced, not diminished, by letting people have a say in how they choose to die. Many of us want the moral and legal right to choose to die with our faculties intact, surrounded by those we love before we are reduced to breathing cadavers with no human dignity attached to our final days. Life must not be identified with the extension of biological existence. [Assisted suicide] is a life-affirming moral choice."

The Catholic belief that suicide is a sin which will cause a person to burn in hell is at the root of the well-financed, virulent opposition to physician aid in dying. This has resulted in expenditures of more than $10 million in losing efforts to defeat the two Oregon initiatives and a successful campaign to defeat the recent Michigan measure. And $6 million was spent in Michigan, most of which came from Catholic donors, to show four TV ads six weeks before voters saw the issue on the 1998 ballot. The ads never attacked the concept of physician aid in dying, but hammered on the well-crafted Proposal B. Surely that money could have been spent to protect life in better ways than to frustrate people who have come to terms with their deaths and want to move on. The arguments that life is sacred and that it is a gift from God rarely are heard now from the opposition. Most Americans do not want to be governed by religious beliefs they don't share, so the argument has shifted to "protection of the vulnerable and the slippery slope." Note, however, that the proposed death-with-dignity laws carefully are written to protect the vulnerable. The request for physician-assisted death must be voluntary, must be from a competent adult and must be documented and repeated during a waiting period. Two doctors must examine the patient and, if there is any question of depression or incompetence or coercion, a mental-health professional can be consulted. After that it must be up to the requester to mix and swallow the lethal medication. No one forces anyone to do anything!

The same arguments were raised in 1976 when the first "living-will" law was passed in California. It again was raised in 1990 when the Supreme Court ruled that every American has the right to refuse medical treatment, including food and hydration, and to designate a proxy to make those decisions if they cannot. This has not been a downhill slope in the last 22 years but an expansion of rights and choices. It has not led to abuse but rather to more freedom. Those who raise the specter of the Nazis must remember that we are in greater danger of having our freedoms limited by religious dogma than of having them expanded so that more choices are available. When the state dictates how the most intimate and personal choices will be made, based on how some religious groups think it should be, then we as individuals and as a country are in serious trouble.

The Benefits of Legalization

One observer said about the Oregon Death with Dignity law: "This is a permissive law. It allows something. It requires nothing. It forbids nothing and taxes no one. It enhances freedom. It lets people do a little more of what they want without hurting anyone else. It removes a slight bit of the weight of government regulation and threat of punishment that hangs over all of us all the time if we step out of line."

Reprinted by permission of George Danby.

Making physician aid in dying legal as a matter of public policy will accomplish several objectives. Right now we have a model of prohibition. There is an underground cadre of doctors—of whom Kevorkian is the tip of the iceberg—who are helping people die. The number varies, according to survey, from 6 to 16 percent to 20 to 53 percent. The 53 percent is for doctors in San Francisco who work with people with AIDS where networks for assisted dying have existed for many years. This practice is not regulated or reported; the criteria and methods used are unknown. There is some information that the majority of these deaths are done by lethal injection. Millions of viewers witnessed on *60 Minutes* the videotape of Kevorkian using this method to assist in the death of Thomas Youk. If the practice is regulated, there will be more uniformity, doctors will be able to and will have to obtain a second opinion and will have the option of having a mental-health professional consult on the case. Most importantly for patients, they will be able to talk about all their options openly with their health-care providers and their loved ones.

Another consequence is that desperately ill people will not have to resort to dying in a Michigan motel with Kevorkian's assistance, with a plastic bag on their heads, with a gun in their mouth or, worse, botching the job and winding up in worse shape and traumatizing their families. They won't have to die the way someone else wants them to die, rather than the way they choose. As Ronald Dworkin said in *Life's Dominion:* "Making someone die in a way others approve, but he believes a horrifying contradiction of his life, is a devastating, odious form of tyranny."

"Wise social policy dictates that some people's wish for physician-assisted suicide cannot outweigh all other effects of its legalization on the many patients who would die inappropriately."

Physician-Assisted Suicide Should Not Be Legalized

American Foundation for Suicide Prevention

In the following viewpoint, the American Foundation for Suicide Prevention (AFSP) states its opposition to the legalization of physician-assisted suicide (PAS). When patients are treated for depression and provided with quality palliative or hospice care, argues the AFSP, they do not request suicide. The foundation cites studies from the Netherlands (where PAS is technically illegal but physicians are not prosecuted for helping patients to die) that report that in about one thousand cases per year, physicians cause the death of patients without their consent. The AFSP concludes that legalizing assisted suicide would endanger far more patients than it would help.

As you read, consider the following questions:

1. In what percent of cases is pain the major reason that patients request suicide, according to the foundation?
2. What position does the American Medical Association take with regard to feeding tubes and other invasive treatments, as described by the AFSP?
3. According to the AFSP, what proportion of Dutch physicians consider it appropriate to propose euthanasia to their patients, and what message do such proposals send to patients?

Excerpted from "AFSP Policy Statement on Physician-Assisted Suicide and Euthanasia," by the American Foundation for Suicide Prevention, www.afsp.org/assisted/policy3.html. Reprinted with permission.

M ost people assume that seriously or terminally ill people who wish to end their lives are different than those who are otherwise suicidal. But an early reaction of many patients to the diagnosis of serious illness and possible death is terror, depression, and a wish to die. Such patients are not significantly different than patients who react to other crises in their lives with the desire to end the crisis by ending their lives. . . .

Recognizing and Treating Depression

Nearly 95 percent of those who kill themselves have a psychiatric illness diagnosable in the months before suicide. The most common mental illness in these suicides is depression, which can be treated. This is particularly true of those over fifty, who are more prone than younger victims to take their lives during the type of acute depressive episode that responds most effectively to treatment.

Like other suicidal individuals, patients who desire an early death during a serious or terminal medical illness usually suffer from a treatable depressive condition. Although pain and other factors such as lack of family support contribute to their wish for death, depression is the most significant factor, and researchers have found it is the only factor that predicts the desire for death.

Both patients who attempt suicide and those who request assisted suicide often test the affection and care of others, confiding feelings like "I don't want to be a burden to my family" or "My family would be better off without me."

Such expressions usually reflect depressed feelings of worthlessness or guilt, and may be a plea for reassurance. They are also classic indicators of suicidal depression in patients who are in good physical health. Whether physically healthy or terminally ill, these patients need assurance that they are still wanted; they also need treatment for depression.

Depression, often precipitated by discovering one has a serious illness, exaggerates the suicidal patient's tendency to see problems in absolute black and white terms, overlooking solutions and alternative possibilities. Suicidal patients are especially prone to setting such absolute conditions on life: "I won't live, . . . 'without my husband,'. . . 'if I lose my looks, power, prestige or health,' or ... 'if I am going to die soon.'" These patients are afflicted by the need to make demands on life that cannot be fulfilled. Determining the time, place, and circumstances of their death is the most dramatic expression of their need for control. ...

The fact that a patient finds relief in the prospect of death is not a sign that the decision is appropriate. Patients who are depressed and suicidal may appear calm and less depressed after deciding to end their lives, whether by themselves or with the help of a doctor. It is coping with the uncertainties of life and death that agitate and depress them.

Unfortunately, depression is commonly underdiagnosed and inadequately treated. Although most people who kill themselves are under medical care at the time of death, their physicians often fail to recognize the symptoms of their depressive illness, or fail to provide adequate treatment. Patients who, fearing illness or death seek death via assisted suicide or euthanasia, may be different from patients who want relief from suffering in their last days. When there is legal sanction for assisted suicide for patients who are not immanently dying, the two groups of patients become hopelessly intertwined and cannot reliably be separated. ...

Patients Already Have the Right to Refuse Unwanted Medical Treatment

Pain is a factor in 30 percent of euthanasia requests, the major reason for the request in about five percent of cases. Pain can invariably be relieved if the physician is knowledgeable about how to do so. Unfortunately advances in our knowledge of how to treat pain has not been accompanied by adequate dissemination of that knowledge. Physicians undertreat even the most severe states of pain based on inappropriate fears of heavy sedation.

Most of the indignity of which patients justifiably complain is associated with futile medical treatments. Doctors are learning to forego such treatment although patients are only beginning to learn that they can refuse them. On the other hand patients are also afraid of being abandoned by their doctors while they are dying. There is basis for these fears since only in the past decade have we begun to educate physicians that caring for patients they can not cure is an integral part of medicine.

There are patients who find it hard to be dependent on others. Yet serious illness usually requires this. Dependency is hardest for patients when their families do not want that responsibility. A change in family attitudes, however, can modify the outcome in cases where patients wish to die. A 1989 Swedish study showed that when chronically ill patients attempted suicide, their overburdened families often did not want them resuscitated. But when social services stepped in and relieved the family's burden by sending in home care helpers, most patients wanted to live and their families wanted them to live, too.

Awareness of the dangers of physician-assisted suicide must be coupled with comparable awareness of the dangers of the unbridled use of life-prolonging medical technologies. It is now accepted practice—supported by the American Medical Association, the courts, and most churches—that patients need not be kept alive by invasive, artificial means, such as by feeding tubes.

With appropriate consent from the patient, family members, or other surrogate decision makers, it is considered the standard of medical care to forgo tube feeding while providing sufficient sedation to relieve any suffering. This is so even though the patient's death is the likely outcome. Patients must be made aware of this option. Doctors must learn when such an approach is appropriate. Hospitals must ensure that patients know that this kind of plan for care and sedation is available when it is appropriate and accepted. . . .

The Dutch Experience

Published literature on the Dutch experience with physician-assisted suicide and euthanasia, as well as the findings of physicians associated with AFSP who have conducted research in the Netherlands on this practice, have persuaded AFSP of the dangers of legalization. . . .

The Dutch experience illustrates how social sanction promotes a culture that transforms suicide into assisted suicide and euthanasia, and encourages patients, family, and doctors to see assisted suicide and euthanasia—intended as an unfortunate necessity in exceptional cases—as almost a routine way of dealing with serious or terminal illness.

The Dutch government-sanctioned studies of assisted suicide and euthanasia done in 1991 and 1995 showed that it was often the doctor, not the patient, who chose to put the patient to death. The investigators used the euphemism "termination of the patient without explicit request" to describe both cases of non-voluntary and involuntary euthanasia.

The Slippery Slope

In theory, the hastened death of Dutch patients is supposed to be a rare event, only to be used in the most intractable cases. In actual practice, however, death-causing "medical" practices have expanded almost geometrically, demonstrating empirically the severe incline of the slippery slope. Thus, today, in Holland, you need not be terminally ill to be killed by your doctor. If you can convince your doctor that your suffering is irremediable, you can experience Death-on-Demand. For example, cases have been documented of an asymptomatic HIV positive man being killed (so much for "living" with AIDS) and a woman who had anorexia. . . .

Despite the guidelines proscribing euthanasia unless specifically requested by the patient, Dutch doctors also engage in involuntary euthanasia. According to a 1991 Dutch Government-sponsored study (the Remmelink Report), more than one thousand people were euthanized involuntarily in 1990. (If the same proportionate number were involuntarily euthanized in the U.S., sixteen thousand per year would be killed without request or consent.) This illustrates a key point usually ignored by euthanasia proponents: Guidelines are mere window dressing to alleviate public fears. The actual practice of euthanasia, once legitimized, is soon virtually uncontrolled.

Wesley J. Smith, *Heterodoxy*, May/June 1996.

Approximately 130,000 deaths occur in the Netherlands each year. The studies revealed that in about 1,000 cases, physicians actively caused the death of their patients without their patients' knowledge or consent. In about 25,000 cases, physicians made medical decisions that might, or were intended to, end patients' lives without consulting them. In nearly 20,000 of these cases (about 80 percent) physicians gave the patient's impaired ability to communicate as their justification for not seeking consent.

This meant that in 5,000 cases, physicians took actions that might, or were intended, to end the lives of competent patients, without ever consulting them.

An attorney who represents the Dutch Voluntary Euthanasia Society provided an example: a doctor terminated the life of a nun without her consent a few days before she would have died because even though she was in excruciating pain, her religious convictions did not permit her to ask for death.

The needs and character of family, friends, and physicians often play a bigger role than the patient's even when the patient apparently requested or consented to die. In a study of euthanasia in Dutch hospitals, the investigator concluded that the families, doctors, and nurses pressured patients to request euthanasia. A Dutch medical journal noted an example of a wife who no longer wished to care for her sick husband; she gave him a choice between euthanasia and admission to a nursing home. The man, afraid of being abandoned to the mercy of strangers in an unfamiliar place, chose to be killed. The doctor, although aware of the coercion, ended the man's life. The government-sanctioned studies revealed that more than half of Dutch physicians considered it appropriate to propose euthanasia to their patients. They seemed not to recognize that the doctor was also telling the patient that his or her life was not worth living, a message that would have a powerful effect on the patient's outlook and decision. . . .

Public Opinion on Physician-Assisted Suicide

Many people have seen others suffer terribly while dying. When asked, "Are you in favor of euthanasia?" most people reply "yes," meaning that they would prefer painless death over suffering. But when asked, "If terminally ill, would you rather treatment make you comfortable, or have your life ended by a physician?" their responses might be different.

People confuse their support for the right to refuse medical treatment—a right supported by law and by civil and religious leaders—with support for the right to die by assisted suicide or euthanasia. The more people know about the care of people who are terminally ill and the pros and cons of legalizing euthanasia, the less they support legalization. Yet the public is still grossly misinformed. A recent poll indicates that only 61 percent of people are aware that under current law, patients may refuse any and all unwanted treatments. Ten percent of the population believe that the law requires a patient to accept whatever treatment a doctor wants to provide. . . .

A More Humane Option

Patients who request assisted suicide or euthanasia are usually asking in the strongest way they know for mental and physical relief from suffering. When that request is made to a caring, sensitive, and knowledgeable physician who can address their fear, relieve their suffering, and assure them that he or she will remain with them to the end, most patients no longer want to die and are grateful for the time remaining to them. . . .

Wise social policy dictates that some people's wish for physician-assisted suicide cannot outweigh all other effects of its legalization on the many patients who would die inappropriately, just as in the Netherlands. To legalize assisted suicide and euthanasia would truly be what ethicist Daniel Callahan has called "self-determination run amok."

Clearly the wiser, more humane course is to successfully provide good palliative care to terminally ill patients. Advances in our knowledge of palliative care in the past twenty years make clear that care for the terminally ill does not require us to legalize assisted suicide and euthanasia. Our challenge, which can be met, is to bring that knowledge and that care to the critically ill.

Our success in providing palliative care for those who are terminally ill will not only address the suffering of the individual patients, but do much to preserve our social humanity. If we do not provide such care, legalization of assisted suicide and euthanasia will become the simplistic answer to the problem of dying. Euthanasia will become a way for all of us to ignore the genuine needs of terminally ill people.

If the advocates of legalization prevail, we will lose more lives to suicide (although we will call the deaths by a different name) than can be saved by the efforts of the American

Foundation for Suicide Prevention and by all the other institutions working to prevent suicide in this country.

The tragic impact on depressed suicidal patients will be matched by what will happen to the elderly, the poor, and other terminally ill people. Assisted suicide and euthanasia will become routine ways of dealing with serious and terminal illness just as they have in the Netherlands; those without means will be under particular pressure to accept the euthanasia option. In the process, palliative care will be undercut for everyone.

Many people have the illusion that legalizing assisted suicide and euthanasia will give them greater autonomy. The Dutch experience teaches us that legalization of physician-assisted suicide enhances the power and control of doctors, not patients. In practice it is still the doctor who decides whether to perform euthanasia. He can suggest it, withhold obvious alternatives, ignore patients' ambivalence, and even put to death patients who have not requested it.

Euthanasia advocates have come to see suicide as a cure for disease and a way of appropriating death's power over the human capacity for control. In the process, they have derailed constructive efforts to better manage the final phase of life. Our social policy must be based on a larger and more positive concern for people who are terminally ill. It must reflect an expanded determination to relieve their physical pain, to discover the nature of their fears, and to diminish suffering by giving affirmation to the life that has been lived and still goes on.

Periodical Bibliography

The following articles have been selected to supplement the diverse views presented in this chapter. Addresses are provided for periodicals not indexed in the *Readers' Guide to Periodical Literature*, the *Alternative Press Index*, the *Social Sciences Index*, or the *Index to Legal Periodicals and Books*.

Rand Richards Cooper — "The Dignity of Helplessness: What Sort of Society Would Euthanasia Create?" *Commonweal*, October 25, 1996.

John Corry — "Who Is Jack Kevorkian, Really?" *Reader's Digest*, April 1999.

Barbara Dority — "The Ultimate Civil Liberty," *Humanist*, July/August 1997.

Ezekiel Emanuel — "Whose Right to Die?" *Atlantic Monthly*, March 1997.

Faye Girsh — "The Pope Wants to Tell You How to Die: Will You Stand for It?" *American Atheist*, Spring 1999.

John Hardwig — "Is There a Duty to Die?" *Hastings Center Report*, March/April 1997.

Leon R. Kass and Nelson Lund — "Courting Death: Assisted Suicide, Doctors, and the Law," *Commentary*, December 1996.

Robert B. Mellert — "Cure or Care?: The Future of Medical Ethics," *Futurist*, July/August 1997.

John Bookser Feister — "Thou Shalt Not Kill: The Church Against Assisted Suicide," *St. Anthony Messenger*, June 1997.

Nancy Shute — "Death with More Dignity," *U.S. News & World Report*, February 24, 1997.

John Shelby Spong — "In Defense of Assisted Suicide," *Human Quest*, May/June 1996.

Adam Wolfson — "Killing Off the Dying?" *Public Interest*, Spring 1998.

CHAPTER 3

Is Abortion Ethical?

Chapter Preface

One and one-half million abortions occur in the United States each year, with 16,000 due to pregnancies caused by rape or incest. While many pro-life activists argue that the fetus should never be aborted, no matter how it was conceived, others agree with supporters of abortion rights that rape and incest are two acceptable reasons for permitting an abortion.

Supporters of abortion rights argue that a woman who is not allowed to end an assault-induced pregnancy effectively endures a second attack, with society and the fetus now the assailants. Judith Jarvis Thomson encapsulated this view in her essay "A Defense of Abortion." She uses the analogy of a person who is kidnapped and awakens in a hospital bed with a renowned violinist attached to his or her circulatory system. The violinist must remain attached for nine months in order to survive. Thomson likens this situation to pregnancy by rape and asserts that just as the hospitalized person is not morally obligated to save the violinist's life, neither should society compel a rape victim to complete her pregnancy. Pro-choice supporters further argue that raising a child that was conceived by rape or incest worsens the woman's trauma. As one woman explains: "The first time that [child] showed hostility or anger or violence, I would say, 'My God, it's going to be just like him, that terrible man.' I would probably raise a child that I was afraid of. Wouldn't that be terrible?"

Pro-life activists counter that abortion, not pregnancy, constitutes a second assault. In his essay "Rape, Incest and Abortion: Searching Beyond the Myths," David C. Reardon asserts that abortion and rape are both invasions of a woman's body. He writes: "The difference? In a sexual rape, a woman is robbed of her purity; in this medical rape she is robbed of her maternity." Abortion opponents also maintain that raising a child that was conceived through sexual assault can help the woman recover. Olivia Gans and Mary Spaulding Bach report in the *National Right to Life News* that "[assault victims] in one study who carried their babies to term . . . felt they had turned something awful into something good."

Abortion is one of society's most controversial issues. In the following chapter, the authors debate the ethics of abortion.

"Abortion is a positive decision and not a lesser evil."

Abortion Is Ethical

John M. Swomley

Abortion is an ethical and moral decision, John M. Swomley asserts in the following viewpoint. He rejects the view that abortion is an act of violence toward another human being, arguing that embryos and fetuses are not yet babies and are unable to feel pain. In addition, he maintains that abortion is a positive moral choice because it gives women control over their lives and fertility. Swomley is an emeritus professor of social ethics at the St. Paul School of Theology in Kansas City, Missouri.

As you read, consider the following questions:
1. What are the two types of abortion, as stated by Swomley?
2. What is "prolepsis," according to Swomley?
3. According to the author, why is the anti-abortion movement wrong to assert that abortion is psychologically damaging?

Excerpted from "Abortion as a Positive Moral Choice," by John M. Swomley, *Human Quest*, July/August 1999. Reprinted with permission.

The violent arm of the right-wing anti-abortion movement is having a field day in the United States, not only with violence against doctors and clinic workers, but now with anthrax threats and hoaxes. At least twenty abortion clinics and other buildings nationwide received anthrax threats in February 1999.

Clinics Are Threatened

The following description in the February 23, 1999, *Kansas City Star* indicates what happens when such a threat is received: "Emergency workers, more than 100 strong, swarmed over the Planned Parenthood clinic in midtown on Monday; hazardous material technicians laboring in white safety suits, police diverting traffic for blocks around the clinic, firefighters and rescue workers pouring in from four cities.

"Inside the clinic 27 persons were stripped and scrubbed with a mixture of bleach and soap, all the result of an anonymous letter" which "contained a note . . . stating that the person reading it had just been exposed to anthrax."

In 1997 "Kansas City was part of the first group of cities to receive new training against terrorism, including anthrax threats. The city has gathered millions in federal grants to train emergency workers and buy special equipment." So when there is a threat, even a hoax, the people who make such threats absorb the resources of the city, traumatize patients and staff, and inconvenience and terrorize a larger group. "For about five hours 47th Street became choked with emergency workers."

"If anthrax spores are inhaled, the bacteria they produce can cause death." At the office of Planned Parenthood in Kansas City, "only one employee, wearing gloves and a mask, opens the mail in an isolated room."

In November 1998 an administrative office of the United Methodist Church in Wichita, Kansas, received a letter threatening anthrax exposure. Also that month, eight abortion clinics in four Midwestern states, including one in Wichita, received similar letters, all hoaxes.

It is a sad fact that the FBI and the Department of Justice never took seriously the violence against clinics and doctors until the October 23, 1998, murder of Dr. Barnett Slepian.

It is also sad and even startling that the Catholic bishops and right-wing Protestant leaders, with an exception or two, have remained silent and have not urged their followers to respect the life of those with whom they disagree. The bishops' 27-page statement, "Living the Gospel of Life," in which they instructed American Catholics to put pressure on and vote only for anti-abortion politicians, was issued in November 1998, a month after Dr. Slepian was assassinated and well after others were killed. Warnings against such violence could easily have been included.

Right-wing columnist Cal Thomas blamed the killing of Dr. Slepian on the cheapening of life by legal abortion. He specifically blamed the *New York Times* "and other defenders of . . . abortion that contribute to the cheapening of life." (*Kansas City Star*, Oct. 30, 1998)

This is now a familiar theme of the anti-abortion movement. Following the Kansas City anthrax scare at the Planned Parenthood clinic, the Western Region coordinator of Missouri Right to Life, in a viewpoint piece in the *Kansas City Star*, first expressed her "abhorrence of violence outside the abortion clinics." Then she launched into an attack on abortion, saying they wondered whether the violence "was set up by the abortion industry to look like the work of pro-life activists." Though she said she did not now believe that, she led readers to suppose it is plausible. She also said, "There is an axiom that violence begets violence," and referred to "the 36 million unborn babies destroyed by the violence of abortion."

Types of Abortion

Some religious groups believe that human beings exist at conception. The fertilized egg, however, is microscopic and weighs a fraction of an ounce, has no body, brain, nor sex, which develop later. It does not implant in the uterus for some days after fertilization. There is no violence in a pill or other medical device that prevents implantation.

Millions of fertilized eggs are discarded by Nature or God and never implant. Up to 50 percent of those that implant are aborted naturally, but called miscarriages. Presumably abortion opponents do not claim God engages in violence or murder. Certainly Catholic theologians such as Augustine and St. Thomas Aquinas never assumed that a person or soul exists at conception.

Abortions after implantation are of two kinds: one is medically induced by a pill, and the other surgically induced, in each case with the request and consent of the woman. Most of us do not believe consensual medical or surgical action is violence.

Abortion Is a Private Matter

I believe that the killing of human life in abortion is different from the killing that occurs in war and in capital punishment. Becoming pregnant is a personal and private matter, and dealing with the pregnancy is also personal and private. The killing that occurs in the other two instances is state sanctioned, ordered, and controlled. I see no inconsistency in the beliefs of those Friends [Quakers] who support the right to private decisions regarding reproductive choice, which may or may not mean abortion in any particular case, but who abhor state-ordered war and state executions of human beings.

Jean Malcolm, *Friends Journal*, May 1998.

Legally there are two types of abortion: elective and emergency. An elective abortion, which is chosen by the woman, must take place in the first trimester (within twelve weeks of pregnancy) or in the second trimester before viability. Physicians performing second trimester abortions must first determine that the fetus is too underdeveloped to survive outside the womb. After 24 weeks (the beginning of the third trimester) the procedure is not elective but emergency, in that the fetus is gravely or fatally impaired, or the woman's life or health is at risk. Ninety percent of abortions are performed in the first trimester, and 99 percent within 20 weeks or before viability.

Abortion Is Not Violence

Because the fetus feels no pain, a function of the brain as yet undeveloped, and the woman acts under her own will and conscience, it is still not violence to a human being.

It is the violent language such as "baby killer" that seems to motivate the violent wing of the right-to-life movement. However, an embryo or fetus is not yet a baby or child. This is a propaganda device known as *prolepsis*, which *Webster's Dictionary* defines as "describing an event as if it has already happened" when in fact it may be months away or never happen. An acorn, for example, is not yet an oak tree, and crushing an acorn is not the same as cutting down a 20- or 40-year-old tree.

It is not enough to say that abortion is not violent. Abortion is a positive decision and not a lesser evil. It gives women control over their lives, their fertility, their education, their vocations, and their responsibility to their families, and is therefore pro-family and pro-life. A book by Patricia Lunneborg, *Abortion: A Positive Decision*, confirms this in eleven chapters, one of which is, "Abortion, Education and Careers."

Adoption Is Not a Viable Option

The anti-abortion movement goes to great lengths to suggest that abortion is a psychological hazard, and urges women instead to give up unwanted children for adoption. Two studies demonstrate the fallacy of these ideas. A panel report published April 10, 1990, in the journal *Science* and commissioned by the American Psychological Association was the result of research to determine if a valid conclusion could be drawn about post-abortion psychological effects. The panel surveyed more than 200 studies and found only about 19 or 20 that met solid scientific standards of investigations.

Their conclusion: "The weight of the evidence from scientific studies indicates that legal abortion of an unwanted pregnancy in the first trimester does not pose a psychological hazard for most women." The greatest distress it found "is likely to be before the abortion." The report also revealed that most women said they had feelings of relief and happiness after an abortion in the first trimester. (*New York Times*, April 6, 1990)

On the other hand, mothers forced to give up their children for adoption have serious problems. The April 16, 1998, *Reporter Dispatch* of West Chester, NY, reported an historic

Catholic mass in Buffalo, believed to be the first "Healing Mass." It was co-sponsored by the Diocese's Pro-Life Office and another group. The report said, "Mothers forced to give up their children not only suffer a sense of loss, but also guilt 'from not being able to tell your child you did not want to give him away. You need your child's forgiveness.'"

The conclusion is not only that abortion is a positive moral choice for an unwanted pregnancy but that it is essential for its defenders to broadcast its positive nature. It is a mistake to let those opposed to abortion create from unproven data the idea that abortion is immoral and violent. It is pro-life for the woman and her family, and demonstrates that American society cares about the health and welfare of women, who otherwise would be subject to compulsory pregnancy with all its risks, if this country again made abortion illegal.

"Abortion is the willful destruction of a potential human life, and that's wrong."

Abortion Is Unethical

Heather King

In the following viewpoint, Heather King, a woman who has had three abortions, explains why she now believes the procedure is not ethical. King explains that her decision to abort was based on selfish reasons, such as her unwillingness to disrupt her life and adopt a less extravagant lifestyle. According to King, her changed view was influenced in part by the works of Flannery O'Connor, a twentieth-century American author famous for her portrayal of Southern life. King contends that abortion is evil because it is an act of violence and profanes the act of procreation. King is a Los Angeles–based writer and former lawyer.

As you read, consider the following questions:
1. According to King, how was her life like a prison sentence?
2. In the author's opinion, why is it wrong to justify abortion on compassionate grounds?
3. What reason for abortions does King think is a dubious proposition?

Excerpted from "One Woman's Journey: Following My Own Unguided Will," by Heather King, *Commonweal*, May 3, 1996. Copyright ©1996 by the Commonweal Foundation. Reprinted with permission. For subscription information, call 1-888-495-6755.

I come from a white working-class family in which I was the first ever to complete college. Coming of age in the '60s, I believed passionately in sexual freedom and the concomitant right to choose abortion. Also a staunch supporter of drinking and drugs, I became deeply alcoholic and sobered up in my mid-thirties to discover that I had somehow graduated from law school. I have now been married for six years, and, at forty-three, am childless. It is difficult to admit that two of the babies I aborted were conceived with married men, one of whom was a one-night stand, and that the third abortion was performed during the course of a long-term relationship. I would like to be able to say that I agonized over the decisions, but the fact is that they were based on expedience and fear. Motherhood would have disrupted my life in every conceivable way. It would call upon resources I was not at all certain I possessed—patience, selflessness, the ability to go without sleep—and I viewed it, frankly, as a kind of prison sentence. It seemed inconceivable that a woman would actually invite the upheaval that a baby entails. I don't care *how* much joy they say it brings, I said to myself, no way am I getting sucked into that trap.

When we arrived in Koreatown [a Los Angeles neighborhood], I was working as a litigation attorney in a Beverly Hills office. I could scarcely have been more temperamentally ill-suited for the job, but it was the first time in my life I had made decent money and I was desperately afraid to give it up. My eyes, red-rimmed with fatigue, fell upon the bimonthly paycheck with the same grim relish a buzzard displays for carrion; I dragged through each day consumed by anxiety and the hideous fear that I would contract some stress-based disease and keel over dead at my desk. I couldn't quite put my finger on it, but there was something fundamentally artificial and dishonest and life-diminishing about the lawyering I was doing. Part of it was the fact that the basic object of litigation is to manipulate the truth, rather than bring it to light; but it also had something to do with the stomach-turning arrogance that prevailed among my colleagues, a presumption of entitlement and innate merit that was doubly repulsive because of the lack of even a rudimentary moral compass.

Reaching Awareness

During those four years my life felt, oddly enough, like a prison sentence—the sentence I had hoped to avoid by exercising intelligence backed by the unfettered exercise of free will. As a matter of fact, although I had enjoyed virtually every purported freedom that modern life has to offer, I realized that in one way, my life had *always* felt like a sentence. I had drunk and smoked and slept around to my heart's content, yet the apotheosis of my personal freedom had consisted of servitude to a bottle of booze and getting pregnant by someone whose name I barely knew. My expensive legal education had bought me a different kind of bondage: in the name of what was supposed to be truth, I took advantage, at least vicariously through my employer, of the opportunity to lie, cheat, steal, bully, lord it over the rest of the peons, and rake in the cash.

This awareness crept over me slowly, in the context of, and strongly abetted by, a religious conversion. It was a long, arduous process, which, though I didn't know it at the time, began the day I stopped drinking. The devil is very much a going concern in the life of an active alcoholic; he is cast out by slow degrees. But the small sense of wonder that accompanied the first blush of freedom from physical dependence was the mustard seed from which everything grew.

The Influence of Flannery O'Connor

One of the people who helped me was Flannery O'Connor. O'Connor lived a monkish life that looked like a kind of penance, but her outlook was breathtakingly devoid of self-pity; in fact, she was dryly, hilariously funny. She wrote—a goal to which I had always aspired and had never done a single thing to advance—with a fierce and uncompromising passion that encompassed and reflected her entire existence. O'Connor saw her writerly vocation as pure grace, once remarking of a trip to Lourdes, made for the ostensible purpose of restoring the use of her legs, that she would rather be able to write than walk.

I had followed my own unguided will, and it had led me straight to hell on earth: an existence characterized by guilt, shame, doubt, insecurity, and the inability to love or be loved.

I lived the kind of violence that appears so inexplicable yet real in O'Connor's stories. And seemingly against every rational instinct, the violence prepared the way for that freedom from the bondage of self that can only be achieved in seeking Christ's will, not our own.

While I could never quite decide whether life in Koreatown was a blessing or a curse, I increasingly began to see that it was the same combination of the grotesque and sublime for which Christ had died and that O'Connor captured in the beauty of her strange and startling stories. Tentatively, I began to attend Mass and study Scripture. I read Thomas Merton, Henri Nouwen, Romano Guardini, Saint Augustine, each of whom helped, in his own way, to introduce me to a new way of looking at and being in the world. The church's opposition to abortion, however, seemed an insurmountable stumbling block. I still could not see how any intelligent, progressive woman could seriously subscribe to the notion of depriving herself of the right to make choices about her own body.

Abortion Is Wrong

But the more I thought about it seriously the more I found that much of the public debate centers on semantics: around "viability," trimesters, whether a finned creature with a shadowy spine is or is not yet "human," the legal definition of murder. These are questions that can go whichever way the wind blows and will never be fully resolved to everyone's satisfaction. Still, sooner or later everyone is forced to agree that scraping off or sucking out whatever you choose to call the living creature in a mother's womb is an act of violence—defined by *Webster's* as "acting with or characterized by great physical force, so as to injure or damage." Abortion is an exercise of power by the strong over the wholly weak. The women's movement has been on the bandwagon for years about the issue of power and exploitation—as it pertains to *men*. Yet jeremiads against violence, I came to think, eventually ring hollow when we resort to violence ourselves.

Nitpicking about whether a fetus somehow "equals" a human being misses the point; what matters is that abortion is the willful destruction of a potential human life, and that's wrong. Abortion profanes the most mysterious act of creation we can know on this earth. It's emblematic of the distorted orientation of our hearts and minds: the faithless heart that makes women want to emulate the "freedom" of the men who have abused or abandoned them.

Fetuses Are Human Beings

We may seek moral shelter behind claims that [the fetus] is not *really* a human being, that it is only a potential human being, that it does not look like a human being. But we know that nothing that is not a human being has the potential of becoming a human being, and nothing that has the potential of becoming a human being is not a human being. We hold against it that it is totally dependent, but it will be as dependent one month outside the womb as it is one month inside the womb. Nor can we entirely repress the knowledge that, in the moral tradition that formed our culture, the condition of dependence obliges others to be dependable. As for it not looking like a human being, the embryo or fetus, or call it what we will, is exactly what a human being looks like at that age. It is what each of us looked like when we were that old.

First Things, January 1998.

Women are wrong if we think that the right to abortion gives us the same kind of "autonomy" men supposedly enjoy. It won't because it can't: in the worst-case scenario, the guy walks away, but we destroy the human life that's growing inside us. We must first recognize that the freedom to deny responsibility for one's actions—whether the actor is a man or a woman—is really no freedom at all. The freedom to choose cannot mean the freedom to choose evil. Above all, the violence implicit in the act of abortion is directed not only against our children but against ourselves; women are implicated physically, mentally, and spiritually in the act of human creation—or its destruction—in a way men cannot be. That is an inexpungable fact of life; instead of being grateful, it seems to piss women off.

Many people justify abortion on compassionate grounds, saying they don't want to bring a child into a world that doesn't share their own sense of compassion. The vague notion underlying my abortions, and I suspect of the vast majority of other women's as well, is the idea that *there wouldn't be enough to go round*—not enough time, not enough energy, not enough space, not enough people to help. But when I examined my motives honestly, I realized that though I *said* not enough for the kid, I *meant* not enough for me. I mouthed platitudes about the global population boom; in fact, I was most worried about overcrowding in my own bedroom. I chafed against the "enforced labor" of motherhood while accepting without question the prevailing consumer ethic that sentences the vast majority of us to a lifetime of economic servitude. The truth in my case is that there was not only enough to go round, there would probably have been more than most of the rest of the world will ever enjoy: maybe not an expensive home or fancy cars—I don't have those things now—but nourishing food and a roof over our heads and comfortable clothes. There would have been books and music and museums. It would have meant sacrifice, deferred plans, missed vacations, no slipcovered down sofa, no hundred-dollar shoes, but there would have been enough. The truth was that I simply did not want to share.

Questionable Justifications

My sense of neurotic guilt is as highly developed as anyone else's. In the course of renouncing my own sins, I know I run the risk of romanticizing the virtues of others. I am attracted, for instance, to the starry-eyed view that every mother is fully conscious of having safeguarded a great mystery and, in the care and education of her child, will continue to do so. I tend to stereotype the Mexican women in my neighborhood as being "natural" mothers and caretakers, with the ability to sacrifice running in their blood. "I have different genes," I tell myself. "I come from a different culture. . . ." This is as far removed from reality and just as wrongheaded as saying that every woman who has an abortion is selfish and irresponsible. The truth is that each of us is a combination of various moral strengths and weaknesses, which is precisely why all need to be held to the same standard. I can't ask for an exception because I think, erroneously or not, that caretaking and doing without are inherently easier for some other group of women, just as the woman with less money or fewer resources can't ask for an exception because some other people have more.

I heard a female physician from Wisconsin gleefully relate how she couldn't pass up the offer to become an abortionist because she came from the land of Senator Joe McCarthy. The irony, she said, was too delicious. But, in fact, there is no irony, just sad proof that violence, whatever form it takes, always begets more. The doctor went on to say that there was really only one reason that women get abortions: it just wasn't time. The majority of the women who came into her clinic had been anti-abortion—until they got pregnant—which, she noted, put them in a "terrible psychological bind." It occurred to me that the bind was rather more spiritual than psychological, and that having an abortion was an odd way to resolve it. Concluding that it isn't time now presumes that somewhere down the road it will be time. The idea that killing an unborn child now will contribute to the parenting skills you hope to develop in the future is a dubious proposition.

Still, the hearts of these women were in a better place than where mine had been: my feeling was that the time to disrupt *my* life would *never* be right. To be honest, I often still feel that way. But I have also come to believe that there is an invisible dimension where the smallest act of creation, or love, holds us together; where destruction, no matter how it is rationalized, or what it is called, inevitably tears us apart. I am convinced, for instance, that if Flannery O'Connor hadn't faithfully sat at her desk writing four hours a day, day after day, every week of her adult life, even when swollen and crippled with pain, that I would not have finally quit my job as a lawyer so I could write, would not have agonized over this essay, would not have recently been received into the Catholic church. There is something unimaginably, mysteriously powerful at work that is called, I'm told, the Communion of Saints.

New Convictions

If I discovered today I was pregnant, I hope my convictions would be steadfast and unwavering. I hope I would know enough to weigh my fear—of birth defects, of making do with less, of not being a good parent, of noise and anxiety and lack of sleep—against the possibility that a child would change me in ways I cannot imagine, in aspects of my life that probably desperately need changing. I hope that I would be so filled with joy and anticipation and wild, abandoned love for the life inside me that it wouldn't occur to me for a second to destroy it. I hope so, but I can't be sure. And although part of my faith is believing I've been forgiven, what I have to live with is the knowledge that three times I forfeited the opportunity to receive the very kind of transforming grace I long for now with all my heart—because I didn't think it was time.

At Jon's Grocery on Eighth and Normandie the other day, a dark-skinned woman with wide hips, short legs, and a shopping bag on each arm, waited patiently while her shrieking little boy took a twenty-five-cent ride on a mechanical horse. Two other children with dirty faces tugged on either side of her skirt, one dripping ice cream, the other waving a toy gun. We had each made our choices, the Latina mother and I, and though the cries of a hungry brat will never wake me, I couldn't help but wonder which one of us rests easier in the long, noisy nights.

> *"Only [the woman] is in a position to determine whether or not she is able or prepared to take the strain involved in raising a severely handicapped child."*

Aborting a Handicapped Fetus Is Ethical

Ann Bradley

In the following viewpoint, Ann Bradley asserts that a woman who aborts a fetus that has a handicap such as Down's Syndrome is making an ethical decision. Bradley argues that since the woman would be responsible for raising the handicapped child, only she can decide whether to bring the pregnancy to term. In her view, doctors and policy makers should not weigh the theoretical interests of the fetus against the real rights of the mother. Similarly, Bradley believes that since the fetus is not a person, fears that abortion of handicapped fetuses will lead to euthanasia of handicapped children or adults are groundless. Bradley is a writer for *Living Marxism*, a British magazine that covers a variety of cultural, moral, medical, and scientific issues.

As you read, consider the following questions:

1. Why does the author think that late abortion due to fetal handicap is an ideal issue for the anti-abortion lobby?
2. According to a study cited by Bradley, what percentage of women who are carrying a fetus with Down's Syndrome choose to continue the pregnancy?
3. In Bradley's opinion, what type of abortion law do women in the United Kingdom need?

Excerpted from "Why Shouldn't Women Abort Disabled Fetuses?" by Ann Bradley, *Living Marxism*, September 1995. Reprinted with permission from *Living Marxism*.

These days there is not much support for anti-abortion arguments *per se*. Even old fashioned moralists like Victoria Gillick hesitate before saying that women should be prevented from having abortions—they prefer to argue that such women are damaged victims of a promiscuous society. But once the issue of fetal handicap is raised, everything seems to change.

The Fetal Handicap Controversy

Many pro-choice activists who defend women's right to end accidental, unwanted pregnancies gag when asked if a woman should be able to terminate a pregnancy—not because she does not wish to have a child, but because she does not want to have a *disabled* child. Indeed even many of those who lobby for abortion on request in early pregnancy see late abortion on the grounds of fetal handicap as a form of discrimination against disabled people—"disability cleansing". This makes it a perfect issue for the anti-abortion lobby to take up. There is little ground for them to gain in arguing against early abortion, which is now acceptable to the overwhelming majority of people. But when the antis take the argument into the territory of late abortion on the grounds of fetal handicap they find that even many pro-choice activists are prepared to make concessions.

Allowing a healthy woman to have an abortion purely on the grounds that her fetus is handicapped smacks of a number of things which many liberals find unacceptable. It is judgmental and value-laden because, in opting to end the pregnancy, the woman says that while she was keen to raise an able child she is not prepared to raise a disabled one. In deciding to abort an abnormal fetus a woman is clearly saying that although she wanted a child, she does not want one on the terms that nature has offered. There are many who find it difficult to accept that some women should seek to take control of their own destiny at the expense of a handicapped fetus.

Medical Viability

Even members of the medical profession now say that they are finding the moral issue "difficult" to resolve, especially with developments in fetal medicine which allow, and encourage, doctors to take action in respect of a fetus. For some doctors, these developments have led to the perception that the fetus is a patient like any other and the subject of medical intervention in its own right. It may be difficult for doctors to accept that, while they are struggling to maintain fetal life at 28 weeks gestation on one day, they can be called upon to end it on the next. The Royal College of Obstetricians and Gynaecologists has commissioned a working party to make specific recommendations on the issue of abortion on the grounds of fetal handicap, and it is being hotly debated in the pages of respected medical journals. Already [in 1995] the prestigious *British Journal of Obstetrics and Gynaecology* has carried two articles calling for a reassessment of current abortion law in accordance with changed views on disability.

Women's Choices Are Attacked

[Reproductive] technology does offer a double-edged sword. Barbara Katz Rothman, who has extensively explored its implications for women, argues that in gaining the choice to abort less than perfect fetuses, women are at the same time losing the choice simply to accept babies in whatever condition they come. Yet to say that because the potential is there to abuse the technology, women must therefore reject it and the choices it offers, wholesale, is to endow the technology itself with a kind of magic, instead of recognizing that the pressures come from the politics of medicine and motherhood, which determine how the technology is applied.

Whatever women choose, they are vilified from one direction or another. If they refuse tests or abortion they are seen as irresponsible, especially by doctors. A woman choosing abortion for reasons of a fetal abnormality gets attacked from other quarters. She is accused of selfishness for her willful refusal to sacrifice herself to care of a baby with disabilities.

Janet Hadley, *Abortion: Between Freedom and Necessity*, 1996.

In June 1995, three eminent professors argued that once the fetus is viable (i.e., once extra-uterine life could be sustained, if necessary with the aid of technology—usually accepted to be 24 weeks gestation), it should be considered a patient in its own right and one towards which the doctor has a "beneficence-based responsibility". These three very eminent professors argue that abortion in the third trimester should be ethically impermissible, unless the fetus has a serious abnormality that can be diagnosed with certainty and which involves an early death or absence of cognitive developmental capacity. This would rule out abortion for conditions such as Down's Syndrome or spina bifida, where neither death nor absence of cognitive developmental capacity can be defined as a certain or near certain outcome.

The acceptance of the fetus as a patient in its own right to which the doctor had specific obligations would be significant, because it would attribute a form of personhood to the fetus, something which it does not yet possess in British law. Although the notion is creeping into American legal definitions, it has been resisted by the British medico-legal establishment for very good reasons.

Even after it reaches the 24-week stage of viability, the fetus does not have a life of its own independent from the woman who carries it. The fetus cannot be understood to possess "autonomy". However, actions taken in the supposed "interests of the fetus" may well infringe the very real autonomy of the woman carrying it. Such actions may even cause her serious harm if they involve clinical intervention against her wishes, or the denial of clinical intervention that she requests—such as an abortion. Few British doctors or legal experts want to be in the position of some of their American colleagues in presiding over forced Caesarean deliveries, or dealing with cases where pregnant women have been imprisoned to prevent them acting in such a way as to possibly harm the fetus.

A Woman's Decision

So far, the majority of medical opinion in the UK has clung to the notion that it is impossible to separate the interests of the fetus *in utero* from those of the pregnant woman because any decisions taken in respect of the fetus will necessarily affect her. This is as true after viability as before. Doctors treat the fetus at the request of, and on behalf of, the pregnant woman. Consequently when making decisions about late abortions for fetal handicap, most sympathetic doctors act in the declared interests of the woman—the interests of the fetus do not really enter into it.

This is exactly as it should be. It is the woman, after all, who has to take responsibility for the child after it has been born, and so only she is in a position to determine whether or not she is able or prepared to take the strain involved in rearing a severely handicapped child. And the overwhelming majority of women who discover that they are carrying a fetus affected by Downs Syndrome currently choose to have an abortion.

A study by antenatal [prenatal] screening expert Professor Eva Alberman shows that just eight percent of women who discover they are carrying a fetus affected by Down's Syndrome decide to continue the pregnancy. And, many would argue, for good reason. When a woman decides to have a child she has an image of what motherhood will be like and what her child will be like. A severely handicapped child—whatever perspective it has on life—simply is not what she anticipated or wanted. Access to antenatal testing and the option of abortion allows a woman to make an informed decision about the future of her pregnancy—and about her own future.

Why should a woman in this situation be denied the option of ending the pregnancy in abortion? No one, at least in this country, argues that women who wish to have disabled children should have their pregnancies forcibly aborted. The argument centres on whether a woman should be allowed to decide whether to continue a pregnancy which she now finds unacceptable.

The Slippery Slope Argument

Those who campaign against abortion argue that women's choice should be denied because the acceptance of abortion for fetal handicap has a corrosive effect on society. They argue that termination for fetal handicap is a slippery slope to euthanasia for the living handicapped, and that by condoning abortion on these grounds society condones discrimination against handicapped people. But this inexorable logic rests on the assumption that we are incapable of differentiating between our actions in respect of fetuses—potential people—and people themselves. After all, those who believe that abortion is a legitimate end to unwanted pregnancy do not accept infanticide as a way of dealing with unwanted babies or murder as a way of disposing of an unwanted partner. The point about slippery slopes—as John Harris, one of Britain's few professors in ethics with his feet on the ground, puts it—is that we, like skiers, learn to negotiate them.

There is much intense speculation about the quality of life of the disabled, and it is this issue which seems to confuse many members of the medical profession. If a fetus is disabled in such a way that the child will endure a short life of intense pain, then it is more likely that there will be a consensus that abortion is legitimate. Things are seen as less clear-cut if the fetal problem is such that the child, were it to be born, would be able to live with a mental handicap which made it unaware that it was even different from other children. But this argument is only of relevance if you assess the legitimacy of abortion from the point of view of the fetus, rather than that of the pregnant woman who may be less willing to assume responsibility for mental handicap than physical pain. If one assumes that a woman should be able to act on what is right for *her* rather than what is right for the fetus—which is not sentient, conscious or aware that there is such a thing as life or death—then this argument loses all validity. . . .

Those who argue that the current abortion law is riddled with eugenic assumptions undeniably have a point. The law was constructed on the assumption that abortion should be available in circumstances where doctors believe that a woman's capacity for good motherhood is undermined by her health or her circumstances, or that it would be better for society if her child were not born. The current abortion law is not the kind of law that women need. We need access to abortion on request—for whatever reason *we* think is appropriate. But until we have won such a law it is important to defend the access to abortion that current legislation gives us—including access to late abortion for fetal handicap—and to celebrate rather than condemn the use of medical technology that allows women the chance to make a choice.

| "Of the 250,000 Americans currently living with Down's Syndrome, most score in the 'mild to moderate' range of mental retardation. . . . Ought they to have been executed?" |

Aborting a Handicapped Fetus Is Unethical

Gregg L. Cunningham

Handicapped fetuses should not be aborted, argues Gregg L. Cunningham in the following viewpoint. Cunningham profiles George Tiller, a Kansas physician who specializes in late-term abortions in cases where the fetus has birth defects or disabilities such as Down's Syndrome. Cunningham maintains that aborting handicapped fetuses is unethical because many families want to adopt those children and most of the babies grow up to lead independent lives. In addition, he charges that because many of these abortions are performed so late in the case of pregnancy, they are equivalent to infanticide. Cunningham is the executive director of the Center for Bio-Ethical Reform, an organization that promotes prenatal justice and right to life for the unborn, disabled, infirm, and aged.

As you read, consider the following questions:

1. According to statistics cited by the author, what percentage of babies with spina bifida who undergo surgery achieves "normal intellectual capacity"?
2. What does Cunningham find bizarre about post-mortem baptisms?
3. What could be a problematic consequence of the effort to map the human genome, in the author's opinion?

Excerpted from "Wave of the Future?" by Gregg L. Cunningham, *National Review*, November 10, 1997. Copyright ©1997 by National Review, Inc., www.nationalreview.com. Reprinted with permission.

Anyone who wonders whether America still has any sense of moral seriousness should download the website of abortionist George Tiller, accessible at http://www.drtiller.com. After browsing through photos of his "operating suite," you can read Tiller's bland acknowledgment that he kills babies at 37 weeks gestational age. For the arithmetically challenged, that's the ninth month of pregnancy. "Baby," by the way, is Tiller's term; he will even refer to his victim as a "child." More alarming than his abandonment of pretense that fetuses are not human is its failure to provoke discernible public outrage.

George Tiller's Justifications

Tiller is by no means the only abortionist killing near-full-term babies, and there are plenty of other abortionists on the Net. But none of his colleagues showcase their handiwork with such self-promotional audacity. Tiller is either completely contemptuous of public opinion or convinced that the public is beyond caring. Either way, his global ads seem to be reaching their target audience; German and Japanese television teams recently visited his home base, Wichita, in search of interviews concerning the European and Asian women who are making the long journey to engage his grisly services. He recently doubled the size of his abortion clinic, and approximately tripled his killing capacity.

It is difficult to confer clinical respectability on the killing of a neonate, but Tiller takes a shot with the Orwellian term "fetal indications termination of pregnancy." The idea is that certain disorders are so serious that there is no point attempting to prolong the child's life. Among these conditions are several maladies which are not fatal and in fact may be only mildly disabling. Tiller names "encephalocele" (hernia of the brain) for instance, which *The Merck Manual* says "can be repaired, and the prognosis is good for many of these patients." He also cites "hydrocephalus" (water on the brain) concerning which *Diseases of the Newborn*, by Schaffer & Avery, says that with few exceptions "every infant with neonatal hydrocephalus should be treated surgically . . . [and] 86 percent of infants survived following their shunt placement. Of these infants, 46 percent were reported normal on follow-up."

Tiller also matter-of-factly observes that the average age

of the more than a thousand late-term babies he has killed is 27 weeks (or the seventh month of pregnancy). Meanwhile, the neonatal intensive-care unit at Via Christi Hospital in Wichita cares for preemies born at 24 and 25 weeks' gestation. Indeed, babies born earlier than that often survive nowadays; the *New York Times* (May 16, 1997), citing the National Center for Health Care Statistics, reports that approximately 15 percent of babies born at 22 weeks will survive, 25 percent at 23 weeks, 42 percent at 24 weeks, and 57 percent at 25 weeks.

Of course, these babies require intensive care, and Tiller apparently thinks that a baby who can't survive without help is not entitled to survive at all. A story in the *Kansas City Star* (August 26, 1991) quoting Tiller spokeswoman Peggy Jarman said that "elective abortions should be considered acceptable into the 26th week because these fetuses are not capable of surviving outside the womb without artificial life supports. 'You're talking about the difference between natural survival and intensive care. . . .'"

In the same interview, Miss Jarman admitted that "about three-fourths of Tiller's late-term patients are teenagers who have denied to themselves or their families that they were pregnant until it was too late to hide it"; abortions are performed on them with no reference to health problems in either the baby or the mother. Since Tiller's website lists the average age of the mothers on whom he performs his fetal-abnormality abortions as 29 years, there can't be much overlap between these two groups. This admission raises the possibility that Tiller could be killing as many as three healthy late-term babies, being carried by healthy mothers, for each "disabled" child he aborts.

Living with Down's Syndrome

One of the conditions for which Tiller says he "terminates" is Trisomy 21—the scientific name for Down's Syndrome. Yet according to *World* magazine (January 18, 1997), of the 250,000 Americans currently living with Down's Syndrome, most score in the "mild to moderate" range of mental retardation, and most can learn to read, hold jobs, and live independently. Ought they to have been executed?

The Centers for Disease Control and Prevention (CDC) report that in the 1980s, abortion reduced the number of children with Down's Syndrome born to white women over 35 in the metropolitan Atlanta area by about 70 per cent. As someone recently put it, eugenics is still a dirty word but it has become a common practice.

Reprinted by permission of Chuck Asay and Creator's Syndicate.

But don't Down's Syndrome babies put a tremendous strain on other family members? The National Committee for Adoption reports that "there is a waiting list of screened families who want to adopt seriously disabled newborns, including babies born with Down's Syndrome and spina bifida." (The latter disability is also among Tiller's conditions warranting abortion.) Most of the parents who don't want these children could place them for adoption by having them delivered alive at the same point in the pregnancy at which Tiller is killing them.

Even with adoptive homes available, there is no reason to doubt the sincerity of parents who, contemplating the prospect of a severely deformed or retarded child, say they wish "to spare my baby a life of hardship." But how are we to decide what will lead to intolerable hardship? As [columnist] George Will has frequently written regarding his son Jonathan, and as I can attest from the observation of a good friend of mine, people with Down's Syndrome appear to be among the happiest people on the planet. As for babies with spina bifida, an article in the *New England Journal of Medicine* in 1985 said that, following surgery, "72 percent were ambulatory and 79 percent had normal intellectual capacity." [Major league pitcher] Orel Hershiser would have been lost to the world if his parents had known that spina bifida is an "intolerable" condition.

Nor is there much to be said for what on the face of it is a strong reason for aborting: to preserve the health of the mother. In May of 1997 the Board of the American Medical Association approved a report finding that, "Except in extraordinary circumstances, maternal health factors which demand termination of pregnancy can be accommodated without sacrificing the fetus, and the near certainty of the independent viability of the fetus argues for ending the pregnancy by appropriate delivery."

A Lack of Priorities

One reason frequently given for the toleration of large-scale abortion of birth-defective infants is that the cost of caring for them is unmanageable. And certainly, there are many cases in which such costs, if they had to be borne by the family alone, would be crushing. But a recent article in the *New England Journal of Medicine* put the annual figure for the country as a whole at $2 billion. That's less than the $2.3 billion Americans spend each year on chewing gum. The CDC estimates that care for people with Down's costs $1.8 billion per year. That is about half the $3.4 billion we spend each year on cookies.

It is, in other words, a question of priorities—and America's today do not seem to be human-centered. The Pet Industry Joint Council says we spend around $63 billion each year on the acquisition, food, training, grooming, etc. of our pets.

Perhaps more to the point, on May 11, 1997, the Associated Press reported that the San Francisco [Society for the Prevention of Cruelty to Animals] (SPCA) had announced that "no adoptable animal . . . with a treatable disease will be euthanized . . . and it will pay for medical care for an animal with a long-term health problem after it is adopted." Milwaukee, St. Louis, and New York are also taking steps to become "no kill" cities. Somehow I don't expect them within the foreseeable future to become "no kill" cities for human babies.

The Fetus Feels Pain

The euphemism Tiller uses to describe the actual killing of "disabled" children is "premature delivery of a stillborn." Of course, the baby is "born still" because Tiller has injected his heart with a lethal dose of digoxin. Tiller says this ensures that the child "will not experience any discomfort during the procedure." But most people who have suffered a heart attack—which is what occurs in this case—describe it as an excruciatingly painful experience. One is also left to wonder how much "discomfort" is experienced by the many thousands of younger, healthy fetuses Tiller routinely tears limb from limb before he kills them, without benefit of anesthesia.

As Vincent J. Collins, M.D., professor of anesthesiology and author of the textbook *Principles of Anesthesiology* (Third Edition, Williams and Wilkins, 1992) reminds us, neurological structures necessary to feel pain, pain receptive nerve cells, neural pathways, and the thalamus of the brain begin to form eight weeks after fertilization and become functional during the thirteenth week. Collins also teaches that the cerebral cortex is not necessary for pain sensation but even if it were, the *New England Journal of Medicine* (November 29, 1987) reports cortical function in both hemispheres of the brain by twenty weeks. That is much younger than the average "fetal indications" baby Tiller admits to killing.

Actually, the efficiency of the killing process is important to late-term abortionists for reasons quite apart from concern for the pain felt by the baby. In instances where babies have inconveniently survived the abortion procedure, abortionists have undergone criminal prosecution for killing them *outside* the mother's body. Far safer to remove any possibility that they will survive.

There is also a juris precedential reason for the medical world's toleration of widespread abortion. Newborn babies in intensive care pose major legal risks for treating physicians. University of Chicago neonatologist William Meadow reports in the *Pediatrics Electronic Pages* for May 6, 1997, that most U.S. doctors treating premature babies will be sued for medical malpractice at some point in their careers, no matter how competent they are. It must be tempting to refer high-risk, late-term unborn babies for abortion rather than treat them and risk a lawsuit.

Fetal Death Rites

In one of the more macabre sections of his advertisement, Tiller recommends that "couples elect to view or hold the baby after the woman has recovered from the anesthesia." Of course, he concedes that "some couples initially find this a very frightening thought." Indeed.

He also said, in a "Dear colleague" letter dated April 19, 1991, in which he solicited abortion business from referring physicians, that "Patients are encouraged to speak directly to their baby if they wish, and finally to say 'good-bye.' (Not all patients choose to be involved in this process. . . .)" In a 1996 promotional video, Tiller offers patients an opportunity to obtain a "family photo" with them holding their dead baby. He also suggests that, as a memento, they might wish to have a lock of the baby's hair or a fetal footprint.

Even more bizarre is the fact that the Rev. George Gardner, pastor of Wichita's College Hill United Methodist Church and an outspoken Tiller apologist, publicly admits to performing post-mortem baptisms on Tiller's victims. If the deceased aren't babies with souls, what do these parents think they're baptizing? If they are babies with souls, why isn't this infanticide?

Justifying Infanticide

On December 9, 1996, a grand jury in Wilmington, Delaware, handed down first-degree-murder indictments against Brian C. Peterson Jr. and Amy Grossberg for allegedly fracturing the skull of their six-pound-two-ounce newborn baby boy and throwing his body into the trash. Their baby had apparently been born alive. But was his situation materially different from that of babies who are three-fourths born before being killed by "partial-birth" abortion?

Abortion opponents have long used such questions as a way of awakening their listeners to what is going on. The danger is that abortion advocates will turn these questions upside down. In *AMA Prism* (May 1973) Nobel laureate James Watson said, "If a child was not declared alive until three days after birth, then all parents could be allowed the choice . . . the doctor could allow the child to die." Beverly Harrison, professor of Christian ethics at Union Theological Seminary, agrees. In *Policy Review* (Spring, 1985) she said, "I do not want to be construed as condemning women who, under certain circumstances, quietly put their infants to death." As a practical matter, the utilitarian views of Professors Watson and Harrison aren't where we're headed, they're where we are.

And there is no sign that the direction is about to be reversed. One of the darker consequences of the current effort to map the human genome will be withering pressure to test unborn children for genetic predispositions to certain "disabilities." And why should we stop at Trisomy 21 and spina bifida? If, for instance, as is argued by homosexual advocacy groups, there is a genetic component to homosexuality, how many parents will want their unborn babies tested for the operative gene? In China and India, fetuses are already aborted for the defect of being female. And a recent study determined that more than one in ten mothers would abort a child susceptible to obesity.

A Self-Absorbed Community

On April 30, 1997, *USA Today* reported that the city of Brandenburg, Germany, had dedicated a memorial to nine thousand physically disabled, mentally retarded, and other persons deemed "inferior" and "unworthy" by the Thousand Year Reich. They were, as the world grows weary of being reminded, systematically executed in the Nazis' euthanasia program. The former prison building in which the victims were held will now house their memorial. I hope and believe that similar memorials will one day be established in the buildings now occupied by abortionists like George Tiller.

Of course, George Tiller is not the problem. He is only a

symptom. The community is the problem; those who take their children to be killed by him and those who make the killing possible by their silence.

This abomination is allowed to continue because there is a great deal of confusion among people of good will as to the circumstances under which early abortions should be legal. But George Tiller's hubris has stripped us of any excuse for confusion over the killing of near-newborns. Those who defend his infanticide for fear of losing their "choice" are taking self-absorption to new and sickening depths.

| *"Without the right to abortion, women do not possess the right to physical integrity."*

The Right to Abortion Is Central to Women's Freedom

Marilyn French

In the following viewpoint, Marilyn French contends that abortion gives women the freedom to control their bodies, a freedom which women lacked until the twentieth century. She argues that much of the opposition to abortion comes from patriarchal institutions, such as the state and the church, which believe that women should be the property of men. French argues that if abortion is made illegal, men will, through rape, be able to compel women to become mothers. French is a literary critic and author whose works include *The War Against Women*.

As you read, consider the following questions:

1. According to French, what was the punishment for women in ancient Assyria who performed abortions?
2. What is the first principle of patriarchy, in the author's opinion?
3. In addition to abortion, what other right does French believe women need?

Excerpted from "Treason, Abortion, and a Woman's Rights," by Marilyn French, *Free Inquiry*, Summer 1998. Reprinted with permission.

In ancient states like Assyria, fathers had the right to decide whether a newborn infant would live, be killed, or (in some cultures) exposed. However, if women performed abortions on themselves or others, they were subjected to the severest punishment in the Middle Assyrian laws: they were impaled and denied burial. This punishment was otherwise reserved for crimes against the state—high treason or assault on the king.

Institutions—the state, the church, or a corporation—are usually governed by a small group of men, whose primary demand from underlings is obedience, deference to their supreme authority. Regardless of the character of the state, whether it be a tyranny or a democracy, crimes "against the state" were and are considered extremely serious infractions. In all past and present states, treason is the worst iniquity, deserving of the death penalty. But in many past states, women were considered treasonous for acts against their husbands: in Babylon, if a wife caused her husband's death in order to marry another man, she was not found guilty of murder but of treason and was impaled or crucified. Thus for women (but not men) the marital relationship is patently paralleled with the relationship of state and subject.

Why Abortion Is Condemned

To place abortion in its historical context illuminates its underlying meaning to patriarchal thinkers. Abortion is not condemned because it involves questions of life or death. Many states have permitted infanticide, many still sanction execution, and all are willing to see people kill and be killed in wars. If destruction of a living being does not deter states or sects from war, why should destruction of an embryo be a serious matter? Moreover, groups opposed to legal abortion are generally unwilling to provide living children with the means to stay alive.

Patriarchal thinkers and institutions condemn abortion because it involves a woman using her own judgment and treating her body as if it were her own, and not the property of her husband. For a woman to assert the right to use her own reason and to possession of her own body, is, in this thinking, treason. It denies the supremacy of the male, which is the first principle of patriarchy.

Patriarchal institutions are founded on the subjection of women. This is why women's bodies are such important markers in the struggle for human freedom and why the struggle for the right to abortion, once won in the United States, has continuously been attacked by patriarchal institutions, even though many men welcome abortion for their own reasons and many are unconcerned with children once they are born. Unable to overthrow the law allowing abortion, patriarchists are trying to break it down into fragments and make the fragments illegal. But even one such victory would give them a lever to declare the entire law invalid, immoral.

Women's Rights

Without abortion, American women in the late twentieth century would not be helpless: they have won other, somewhat less-contested rights to education, decently paid work, the right to own property, and to be free from physical abuse. Although men do not always respect these rights,

Reprinted by permission of Ann Telnaes.

women can seek recourse through law. But without the right to abortion, women do not possess the right to physical integrity. Since some men are willing to take and use women's bodies and sexual capacities by force, to rape them within marriage or outside it, and, since many women are unable to fight off such male assaults, women must have the power and right to undo what men do—the right, not just to birth control, but to abortion. Unless a woman has both rights—to birth control and abortion—she cannot be sure of maintaining her own bodily integrity.

Men often claim that women are bound by their own bodies, their own "nature": it is women, after all, who get pregnant. But it is not women's, but men's bodies that oppress women. Until the twentieth century, when women won access to reliable birth control and legal abortion, they were bodily bound to men, their victims and pawns. If abortion were illegal, men would in principle regain the legal right to force women into motherhood. This would set back the continuing struggle for human rights by a century.

| *"Women who refuse to accept the 'choice' of abortion also refuse to participate in their own oppression and in the oppression of their children."*

The Right to Abortion Does Not Improve Women's Freedom

Carolyn C. Gargaro

Abortion does not increase women's freedom and autonomy, argues Carolyn C. Gargaro in the following viewpoint. She contends that abortion on demand enables men to have sexual relations without taking responsibility for their actions, and that it has created a culture in which pregnant women are discriminated against. In her view, true feminists value all life, including that of men, women, and the unborn. Gargaro is a web page designer and the manager of several websites.

As you read, consider the following questions:
1. What choices do pro-life feminists want to give women, according to Gargaro?
2. According to Gargaro, how is abortion incompatible with the feminist belief that all humans have inherent worth?
3. In the author's opinion, how does abortion liberate employers and schools?

Excerpted from "What is a 'Pro-Life Feminist?'" by Carolyn C. Gargaro, found at www.gargaro.com/lifefem.html. Reprinted with permission from the author.

"Feminist" is a tricky term to use today—many women who are independent, support equal opportunity, and fight against injustices such as rape and abuse would consider themselves feminists. However, today's definition of "feminism" as defined by groups such as the [National Organization for Women] (NOW), reject women who do not fit into their specific and radical idea of feminism. For instance:

> Sue Purrington, exec. dir. of NOW's Chicago chapter, said the following regarding Feminists For Life: "Either they misunderstand the whole issue of feminism, or they are using it for purposes I disagree with. Their philosophy is irrelevant."
>
> Patricia Ireland on Feminists For Life: "Their only agenda is antiabortion work." *Chicago Tribune 11/12/89*

In fact, Feminists for Life of America was founded by two women who were kicked out of NOW due to their pro-life views. A pro-life woman most often is told that she is not, and cannot be, a feminist. I myself have been told such a thing.

Explaining Pro-Life Feminism

True feminism, as I believe, condemns those who support oppression—whether the oppression be against women, men, minorities, or the unborn. Modern feminism has lost sight of the true meaning of feminism in the regards that modern feminism does not acknowledge the value of women who choose to stay home rather than work in the "business" world, or the value of a child if it is in the mother's womb.

Pro-life feminists respect *all* human life, and they do not place their morality on people—including the unborn—by deciding who should live and who should die. Some people call pro-life feminists "anti-choice"—well, pro-life feminists *are* anti-choice, when it comes to abortion. They are also anti-choice when it comes to rape or the abuse of women. No one should have the "choice" to rape or abuse women either. No one should have the "choice" to beat a woman or not.

Pro-life feminists want *real* choice for women. A *real* choice where women have the option to *choose* effective birth control, effective being the key word. A *real* choice when it comes to having a career and a child—women should not be in the situation where they either have an abortion or risk losing their job. What kind of choice is that? And this sort of thing *does* happen. What does this say to women? That a pregnant woman isn't as valuable in the workplace? How is *that* showing a respect for women? How does that type of attitude "liberate" women?

Pro-life feminists reject abortion because they reject the use of violence to solve a problem. They want more than to just settle for mere equality of opportunity—the opportunity to contribute equally to violence and human rights abuses in society. Pro-life feminists seek to transform society to create a world that reflects true feminist ideals.

"True Feminist ideals" are part of a larger philosophy that values all life, including the life of the unborn. Feminists believe that all human beings have inherent worth—a worth which cannot be conferred or denied by someone else.

Abortion Is Not Liberating

Abortion is completely incompatible with this feminist vision. Abortion makes the unborn and the mother enemies, and basically pits women against their own children so women can achieve "equality." For in today's society, women have not achieved true equality—they still must, many times, abort to be on an equal level politically, socially, and in the business world.

This does not mean that men are to blame for all abortions—they aren't. In fact, it is often the men who respect women, the ones who will take responsibility for their actions, and want the woman to keep the child and who will help in the raising of the child, that are seen as the "oppressors." They are the ones seen as controlling women, when in actuality, it is the irresponsible ones that are seen as "compassionate." The men who encourage women to abort, to avoid taking responsibility for their actions are the ones who do not respect women.

Abortion doesn't "liberate" women—it "liberates" men. Abortion on demand liberates men who want sex without strings, promises, responsibility, or the rituals of romance. And if the woman has the baby? Hey, that's her problem. She could have gotten an abortion—she chose to carry the child; let her pay for her choice.

Abortion also "liberates" others—not the pregnant woman.

For instance, employers do not have to make concessions to pregnant women and mothers. Schools do not have to accommodate to the needs of parents, and irresponsible men do not have to commit themselves to their partners or their children.

A Destructive Surgery

Abortion doesn't cure any illness, it doesn't win any woman a raise, but in a culture that treats pregnancy and child-rearing as impediments, it surgically adapts the woman to fit in.

If women are an oppressed group, they are the only group that requires surgery in order to be equal. In Greek mythology, Procrustes was an exacting host: if you were the wrong size for his bed, he would stretch or chop you to fit. The abortion table is modern feminism's procrustean bed. In a hideous twist, the victims actually march in the streets to demand the right to lie on it. I know that unintended pregnancy can raise devastating problems, but legalizing abortion is the wrong solution. By giving women permission to have their children killed, we have let in a Trojan Horse whose hidden betrayal we've just begun to see.

Frederica Mathewes-Green, *The Plough*, Spring 1998.

By accepting abortion, women have agreed to sacrifice their children for acceptance in this "pregnancy limits freedom" society. Many feminists have given in to the standard which permits the treatment of "unequals" unequally, and for the powerful to oppress the weak. Isn't this what feminists fought *against*?

Abortion Is Not a Right

Women who refuse to accept the "choice" of abortion also refuse to participate in their own oppression and in the oppression of their children. Pro-life feminists refuse abortion and all it represents. Pro-life feminists such as myself reject abortion and the idea of dominance that goes with it. Diminishing the value of one category of human life—the unborn—leads the way for the diminishment of the value of all human life.

Do I understand why women support abortion? Yes, I do. I see women discriminated against because they have children; I see women being abused and thus are scared to go through with a pregnancy for fear that the abuser will beat them more; I see women not getting equal job opportunities because they are pregnant or have children; I see women put in poverty because they are left by their partner to care for children alone.

But women should not be in these situations in the first place! Abortion is accepting of the fact that women are not truly equal unless they are "not pregnant." Abortion does not solve the underlying reasons why women often abort in the first place.

In summary, pro-life feminists feel that the "right" to destroy their own offspring is not a "right"—no one has the right to destroy another human being.

Periodical Bibliography

The following articles have been selected to supplement the diverse views presented in this chapter. Addresses are provided for periodicals not indexed in the *Readers' Guide to Periodical Literature*, the *Alternative Press Index*, the *Social Sciences Index*, or the *Index to Legal Periodicals and Books*.

Helen Alvare, Marie C. Wilson, and Naomi Wolf	"Abortion: Whose Values? Whose Rights?" *Tikkun*, January/February 1997.
Anonymous	"I Am an Abortion Doctor," *Ms.*, June/July 1999.
Melanie Conklin	"Blocking Women's Health Care," *Progressive*, January 1998.
First Things	"*Roe*: Twenty-Five Years Later," January 1998. Available from the Institute on Religion and Public Life, 156 Fifth Ave., Suite 400, New York, NY 10010.
Marlene Gerber Fried	"Legal but . . . : Framing the Ethics of Abortion Rights," *Resist*, April 1998. Available from 259 Elm St., Suite 201, Somerville, MA 02144.
Sarah Glazer	"*Roe v. Wade* at 25," *CQ Researcher*, November 28, 1997. Available from 1414 22nd St. NW, Washington, DC 20037.
Deborah Hornstra	"A Realistic Approach to Maternal-Fetal Conflict," *Hastings Center Report*, September–October 1998.
Issues and Controversies On File	"Abortion," December 5, 1997. Available from Facts On File News Services, 11 Penn Plaza, New York, NY 10001-2006.
	"Labor," *Humanist*, January/February 1997.
Robert Jesolowitz (trans. Ron Chandonia)	"Eugenics, Abortion and the Nazis Plan," *Life Advocate*, March/April 1998. Available from PO Box 13656, Portland, OR 97213.
Maclean's	"Beyond Abortion," special section, August 19, 1996.
Michael W. McConnell	"*Roe v. Wade* at 25: Still Illegitimate," *Wall Street Journal*, January 22, 1998.
Peggy Noonan	"Abortion's Children," *New York Times*, January 22, 1998.
Katha Pollitt	"Take Back the Right," *Nation*, March 18, 1996.
Wendy Shalit	"Whose Choice? Men's Role in Abortion Decisions," *National Review*, May 18, 1998.

CHAPTER 4

Is Capital
Punishment Just?

Chapter Preface

On February 3, 1998, Karla Faye Tucker became the first woman to be executed in Texas since the Civil War. She had been sentenced to death after murdering two people with a pickaxe. Her execution followed a prison stay that included a conversion to Christianity and marriage to the prison chaplain. These details of Tucker's post-conviction life caused many people who had earlier supported capital punishment to question whether it is just. Others viewed the controversy surrounding the Tucker case as a sign of hypocrisy, charging that the morality of capital punishment is only questioned when it involves an attractive, religious woman.

Among those who pleaded for Tucker's life were religious leaders Pat Robertson and Jerry Falwell. Robertson wrote that Tucker "is not the same person who committed those heinous ax murders some fourteen-and-a-half years ago. . . . I think to execute her is more an act of vengeance than it is appropriate justice." Tim Chavez, a columnist for the *Tennessean*, maintains that Christian Americans ignored their values by executing Tucker. He writes: "This country of ours—supposedly under God—took the life of someone who bought into what we believe."

People who argued against commuting Tucker's sentence to life in prison maintained that her supporters only found the death penalty abhorrent when it was imposed on a white Christian woman. If capital punishment is to be just, those who supported Tucker's execution contend, then it must apply to both genders equally. Others assert that had Tucker been an unattractive man, her execution would have garnered little attention. In an opinion piece in the *Columbian*, Susan Nielsen writes: "Falwell and Robertson can go back to being staunch supporters of the death penalty. Death-row inmates can go back to being big ugly guys. Easy to hate, easy to ignore."

Karla Faye Tucker's execution was one of the most talked about in recent years. However, the debate over the death penalty began long before her death and is unlikely to end soon. In the following chapter, the authors debate whether capital punishment is just.

| *"The death penalty, when imposed and carried out, is justice."*

Capital Punishment Is Just

David Leibowitz

In the following viewpoint, David Leibowitz asserts that capital punishment is a just penalty for murder. According to Leibowitz, claims by death penalty abolitionists that capital punishment is cruel and unfair are wrong, because the death penalty is the only appropriate response to the most violent and brutal crimes. He contends that the death penalty process could be improved by streamlining the appeals process. Leibowitz is a columnist for the *Arizona Republic*.

As you read, consider the following questions:

1. What were some of the crimes committed by Robert Wayne Vickers while on death row, as listed by Leibowitz?
2. According to the author, how does the Anti-Terrorism and Effective Death Penalty Act help fix the death penalty?
3. In Leibowitz's view, what is the aim of the American system of justice?

Excerpted from "Death Penalty Showdown: It Is Just, Legal, and Supported by a Majority," by David Leibowitz, *The Arizona Republic*, May 16, 1999. Reprinted with permission.

Always, I recall the dead woman's hands. I saw them in a photograph once, not long before I watched her killer die from a dose of poison injected by the state of Arizona.

The woman's name was Amelia Schoville, and in that picture her hands resembled claws, swollen with blood, thumbs bound by a shoelace, fingers straining up from the dirty mattress where she died.

I remembered those hands on the night [in April 1998] when Amelia's killer, Jose Roberto Villafuerte, was put to death, 5,540 days after he killed her. I recalled Amelia's hands again May 5, 1999, when Robert Wayne Vickers finally got a deadly needle after twenty-one years on Arizona's Death Row.

Imagine those hands, ever-empty, ever-reaching. Now, multiply them by every Death Row convict on every Death Row in each of the thirty-eight states that uses the death penalty.

Think of all those victims, all those empty hands. All that justice denied.

The Death Penalty Is Just and Legal

Make no mistake: Although foes of capital punishment will try to cloud this issue by injecting religion or by scrambling after some illusory moral high ground, the death penalty, when imposed and carried out, is justice.

Execution represents a proportional, measured response to mankind's most barbarous act. It has precedent, it has been ruled legal countless times by countless courts, and it is supported by an overwhelming majority of Americans. In a nation where justice is often represented by a set of scales, execution as punishment for a depraved murder marks the ultimate—and only—systemic balance.

Joe Maziarz has spent the past dozen years prosecuting death penalty appeals for the Arizona Attorney General's Office.

"If society is not willing to exact justice, what purpose do we serve for the citizens?" he asks. "If someone had killed my wife, I can't take the law into my own hands. I rely on society to do that.

"For some murders, the only justice, from a societal perspective, is the death penalty."

Case in point: "Bonzai Bob" Vickers.

A one-man crime wave who developed an animal's lust for blood, Vickers first earned a spot on Arizona's Death Row in 1978, for the jailhouse murder of his cellmate, Frank Ponciano.

Feeling wronged because Ponciano had taken his Kool-Aid and failed to awaken him for lunch, Vickers stabbed his victim to death, then carved "Bonzai" into Ponciano's back.

Vickers' lone regret, as told to a prison psychologist? He didn't have time to add a swastika beside the misspelled Japanese war cry.

Four years later, already a resident of Cellblock Six, Vickers somehow managed to top himself. After fellow killer Buster Holsinger made a suggestive remark about a photo of Vickers' eleven-year-old niece, Vickers fashioned a firebomb using hair gel. He burned Holsinger to death, then tossed in a second firebomb for good measure.

"Did I do a good job?" Vickers asked investigators later. "I told them they should have gassed me in December, when they had a chance."

Instead, his execution took an additional seventeen years. That was time enough for Vickers to complete his legend: 158 major violations while behind prison walls, including a dozen assaults on corrections officers, twenty attacks on inmates and forty charges of making weapons.

Foes of the death penalty often argue that execution has no deterrent effect. That may well be true for society at-large—especially given the decades between a crime and an execution—but one thing is certain:

What happened May 5 in the Florence prison permanently deterred "Bonzai Bob" Vickers, who badly needed deterring.

Strengthen the Death Penalty

Another favorite anti-death penalty argument holds at its crux the notion that our justice system is "broken." Death sentences are inconsistently dispensed, say the abolitionists; the decades of appeals represent "cruel and unusual punishment;" the system is not cost-effective. Thus, they say, capital punishment should be abandoned.

Wrong. It should be fixed.

The Anti-Terrorism and Effective Death Penalty Act, approved in 1996 after nearly twenty years of congressional debate on the subject of federal appeals, was a small step in that direction.

The act, with its time limits on filings and judges' decisions, and its limitations on successive federal appeals, has significantly streamlined the judicial process, mostly by cutting down on capital defense lawyers' favorite trick: frivolous claims of mental incompetency.

Nations Must Protect Good Citizens

The whole reason why nations and governments exist is to defend their decent citizens from vicious criminals. When it fails to do that, they become of little use to its citizens. When a society ignores their moral duty to defend the safety and security of their decent citizens and leaves them at the mercy of violent criminals, they are not being "civilized," they are being negligent.

I am certain that there will come a time when all the nations in the world will be forced to agree after decades of experience on this issue, that capital punishment, like the military and the police force and taxes, is an inevitable and unavoidable consequence of every civilized society and it will no longer be a question of whether or not a nation should have the death penalty, but rather how it should be used.

While I believe that prompt and consistent executions would have a deterrent effect, there remains one great virtue, even for infrequent executions. The recidivism rate for capital punishment is zero. No executed murderer has ever killed again. You can't say that about those sentenced to prison, even if you are an abolitionist.

Wesley Lowe, "Pro Death Penalty Webpage,"
http://www.geocities.com/Area51/Capsule/2698/cp.html.

"Usually, it's limited only by the imagination of the defense attorney," Maziarz says. "They shop around for these shrinks that will basically say, based upon these brain scans . . . and looking at this person's background, that they have a 'brain disorder.' . . . It's like trying to grab a hold of Jell-O. There's no way to prove or disprove anything."

The Incompetency Charade

Find a sympathetic federal judge, and the process stops cold, even when guilt or innocence is no longer up for contention.

As proof, look no further than the case of Michael Poland, convicted in 1979, along with his brother, in the killing of two armored-car guards while stealing $288,000.

In October 1998, a federal judge in Hawaii stayed Poland's execution only two hours before its enactment. At the center of his ruling: A defense-team psychologist who claimed the "stress" Poland endured on Death Row left him incompetent for execution.

The amazing thing: Just sixteen days before that psychologist ruled him insane, Michael Poland was sane enough to bribe a prison investigator in a brazen try to escape Death Row.

Assistant Attorney General Paul McMurdie has spent years on the Poland case. I spoke with him hours after the stay.

"(Mental) incompetence like this isn't all of a sudden just going to happen," he told me. "This is nothing but a charade to make sure the execution didn't take place."

And it worked, at least temporarily—Poland comes up for execution again on June 16th, 1999. [He was executed that day.]

Two obvious outcomes of ploys like this: The killer's legal bill soars, while the execution abolitionists rant.

Improve the Appeals Process

"To me, it's like a self-fulfilling prophecy," says McMurdie's colleague, Maziarz. "The anti-death penalty forces try to make it as expensive as possible. They unfortunately convince the courts to spare no expense and no time in allowing all this to keep mushrooming. Then, when they're successful in doing that, they point to that and say, 'Ah ha, look how expensive it is . . . to get someone executed.'"

Again, the answer would appear to lie with repairing the process, with making the death penalty a consistent, certain answer to the worst kinds of murder.

Of course, saying the appeals process needs to be fixed isn't saying it needs to be curtailed: In Arizona, there is no time limitation on convicted murderers making claims of actual innocence, nor should there be. Newly discovered evidence and new facts can be brought forth at any time, even if repeated claims of sudden insanity have been limited.

"The number one thing is making sure that the guilty are convicted and the innocent are not," Maziarz says. "We don't want to execute innocent people."

What we do want to do, instead, is consistent with the aim of the American system of justice: To adequately, proportionally punish those who would violate the code that governs society.

The very worst of us, those like "Bonzai Bob" Vickers and Jose Villafuerte, deserve as much as a consequence. And those like Rick Schoville, a man who waited fifteen years to get justice in the murder of his mother, deserve nothing less.

"It brought a closure to it," Schoville says thirteen months after the fact, "and for that I'm really, really happy. . . . Now that I see more of these people getting executed, I personally think it's about time that's actually taking place.

"I know how I felt, what a relief it was to finally bring that part of it to an end. I can only imagine how victims of these other people must be feeling. These guys are finally getting what they deserve."

As he speaks, I imagine his mother's hands—now untied, now set free, finally getting to touch what had always been just out of grasp.

*"Killing in the name of a 'higher value,'...
is a subtle killing of ethics itself."*

Capital Punishment Is Unjust

John Kavanaugh

The intentional killing of another person, including capital punishment, cannot be justified, John Kavanaugh asserts in the following viewpoint. Kavanaugh contends that capital punishment, as with other murders, violates basic ethical principles because it requires the depersonalization of its intended victims. According to Kavanaugh, no person should be treated as an expendable object. Kavanaugh is a columnist for *America*, a Catholic magazine.

As you read, consider the following questions:
1. What are some of the examples of depersonalization provided by Kavanaugh?
2. What is the "limit situation in ethics," according to the author?
3. How does Kavanaugh view the right to defend oneself?

"There comes a point when a human being has forfeited all claims to being human. Who knows when? But that lump of flesh has ceased to be human and has become a cancer on the body of society and must be killed to help cure the whole."

Depersonalizing the Enemy

Thus ran an argument in favor of capital punishment offered in a letter to the editor published in the *Saint Louis Post Dispatch* in June 1997. It is the classic move of depersonalization that eases a conscience preparing to kill.

From ancient days to our own, this has been done. Non-Greeks were once labeled "barbarians," non-Chinese were "foreign devils," Chinese were "gooks," Germans were "Huns," Jews were "sub-human" in the Nazi primers given to the Hitler Youth, criminals were "vermin," fetuses were "blobs of protoplasm," the comatose were "vegetables," Africans were "savages," Communists were "monsters," capitalists were "pigs," British were "thugs," the Irish Republican Army (I.R.A.) were "moral animals," blacks and women were "property," Amerinds were "brutes."

Of course, these were all humans, despite the efforts at depersonalization. But even the acknowledgement of the enemy's humanity does not stop the logic of death. For the next tactic is to propose that there are certain kinds of humans that may be killed. They may be powerless, sick, unborn, hostile, criminal or threatening. But they must go.

There is always a reason, always a desired purpose for every killing: to defend my life, my name, my property, my family, my heritage, my race, my nation, my religion. In each case, a moral "absolute" is invoked: but it is never the absolute value of human life. The value of a person is the one value that is expendable. There is, after all, one thread of logic that unites the mind of Timothy McVeigh, found guilty of the abominable Oklahoma City terror, with those who seek his death: the view that there are acceptable, even commanding reasons to kill.

This is the constant pattern of evil, whether we eliminate a person or exterminate a people. In every case there is a "higher" value that provides exception to "Thou shalt not kill." Killing in the name of a "higher value," however, is a subtle killing of ethics itself. For in killing persons, the foundation of moral experience is itself violated.

Intentional Killing Is Unethical

To do ethics, to be ethical, presumes a radical affirmation of personal dignity. In every moral choice is an implicit yes to personal existence. But intentional killing of humans is a radical no to personhood. It undercuts the ethical universe itself.

Let me suggest a grounding principle for ethical issues of life and death. Affirmation of the intrinsic value of persons and personal moral dignity require that we never negate the personhood of ourselves or others, that we never treat any person as a mere thing or object. If personal life is expendable, ethics is expendable.

Since killing a person is the definitive act of turning a living human into a dead thing, since such killing is the irreversible negation of a personal life, any ethics that allows it will corrupt ethics—which rests upon personal dignity—from within.

Inviolability of human life is the limit situation in ethics. If we violate it, we violate the moral order and the claims it makes upon us.

Such a moral absolute is, admittedly, a demanding one. This may be why it has always been rejected throughout history when men and women have found it more realistic to declare others dispensable.

The main objection to a principle of non-killing has involved the threat of an unjust enemy, whether criminal or warrior. May I or my family or my nation do nothing if our own lives are at stake? Ought we not give the greatest penalty for the greatest crimes? If we do not, doesn't this degrade our own value?

I propose this: It is a positive moral good to defend oneself. Even more, we may do everything in our power to defend ourselves, short of violating the foundational principle itself by intending to kill the aggressor. Aggression provides no exception. What atrocity in history has not been perpetrated in the name of protection against real or imagined aggressors?

The deliberate will to kill a human is crucial here. The

motive is murder, even if sincerely, courageously, or self-righteously done. Although not all killings of humans are in every way equivalent, they do share one important thing: a reason to kill.

Murder Is Inexcusable

This absolute principle of non-killing is not a recommendation of passivity. Quite to the contrary, a primary commitment to the inherent dignity of personal life drives us to intervene on behalf of the defenseless or the victim. Our only moral limit is the direct intended killing of the aggressor.

The Death Penalty and Disconnection

I believe our society allows the death penalty only because we believe that those on death row are not human like us. The death penalty is possible only when we disconnect from each other.

Joe Doss, an Episcopalian bishop, has pointed out the difference between baptism, a ritual which welcomes a person into community, and execution, which takes a person out of it, step-by-methodical-step. When I accompanied [Patrick Sonnier] to his execution, I witnessed the system we had put in place to remove him from the human community and kill him. It is a secret ritual, done behind prison walls in the middle of the night.

Paul called us the body of Christ. This means that we are *all* connected. We can never say to one another "I don't need you."

Helen Prejean, *Other Side*, September-December 1997.

It was much more the lack of commitment to intrinsic personal dignity that allowed people to stand by passively, not only when Hitler came to power, but also while he destroyed millions. It was Hitler who exploited the rationale of self-defense to justify his own outrages. And most of his followers swallowed his rationalizations of just punishments and just war. Such were the requirements of moral "realism."

Has there ever been a war that was not justified by both sides? Has there ever been an assassination or act of terrorism that has not been rationalized by some logic of self defense? Has there ever been a murder that has not had an excuse? My proposal is that it is always inexcusable.

Too unrealistic and heady, one might say. But a probe of the Gospels might yield a moral law more "unrealistic" and "unreasonable" yet.

"The death penalty is about nothing more than revenge."

Capital Punishment Is Vengeful

Carol Fennelly

In the following viewpoint, Carol Fennelly maintains that capital punishment is about revenge rather than justice. In her view, capital punishment appeals to a cruel "get tough on crime mindset" and ignores the nobler goal of rehabilitating criminals. She observes that although the execution of Karla Faye Tucker changed the views of some religious leaders who had earlier advocated the death penalty, the majority of Americans continue to support capital punishment. According to Fennelly, the United States as a whole has yet to prove it has ended its desire for revenge. Fennelly is the director of communication for *Sojourners*, a progressive Christian magazine.

As you read, consider the following questions:

1. What are some of the criticisms of the United States that appeared in a U.N. Human Rights Commission report?
2. How many executions took place in the United States in 1997, according to Fennelly?
3. According to a survey cited by the author, what percentage of Americans favor the death penalty under certain circumstances?

Excerpted from "To Die For," by Carol Fennelly, *Sojourners*, July/August 1998. Excerpted with permission from *Sojourners*, 1-800-714-7474, www.sojourners.com

[In April 1998,] the world looked on in horror as 22 Rwandans were executed for their roles in the African nation's 1994 massacres that killed at least 500,000. Even more disturbing to the international community was the dancing, clapping, and whooping of the nearly 10,000 on-lookers who turned out for the spectacle. The United States was among the nations speaking out against the punishment.

That same week the U.N. Human Rights Commission issued a stinging report that called for the United States to suspend all executions, saying, "A significant degree of unfairness and arbitrariness in the administration of the death penalty . . . still prevails." The report rebukes the United States for executing people for crimes committed as juveniles and people who are mentally retarded. It also found that race and economics play a major role in determining the severity of sentences. Religious leaders and human rights activists who have long called for doing away with capital punishment hailed the report.

Inmates Are Denied Their Rights

In 1997, 74 executions were carried out in the United States. Consider this:

• Recently in Virginia the execution of a Paraguayan man was carried out in spite of the protests of the World Court, Secretary of State Madeleine Albright, and appeals from around the world. At the time of his arrest, the man had been denied his right to counsel from his embassy.

• In an Arizona case, a Honduran man who had been denied similar rights was executed despite appeals from the president of Honduras.

• A Texas state legislator has introduced legislation that would make children as young as 11 death-penalty eligible. In Pontiac, Michigan, a 12-year-old boy is being tried as an adult for a murder he committed at age 11.

• In Denver, a local radio station called for listeners to drive by the station and honk if they wanted to "fry" Timothy McVeigh. Twenty-four thousand Coloradans did so. A Detroit News columnist hoped he'd catch fire in the chair, writing that "nothing smells better than a well-done mass murderer."

Capital Punishment Is Unjustified Retribution

Justice, it is often insisted, requires the death penalty as the only suitable retribution for heinous crimes. This claim does not bear scrutiny, however. By its nature, all punishment is retributive. Therefore, whatever legitimacy is to be found in punishment as just retribution can, in principle, be satisfied without recourse to executions.

Moreover, the death penalty could be defended on narrowly retributive grounds only for the crime of murder, and not for any of the many other crimes that have frequently been made subject to this mode of punishment (rape, kidnapping, espionage, treason, drug trafficking). Few defenders of the death penalty are willing to confine themselves consistently to the narrow scope afforded by retribution. In any case, execution is more than a punishment exacted in retribution for the taking of a life. As Nobel Laureate Albert Camus wrote, "For there to be equivalence, the death penalty would have to punish a criminal who had warned his victim of the date at which he would inflict a horrible death on him and who, from that moment onward, had confined him at his mercy for months. Such a monster is not encountered in private life."

It is also often argued that death is what murderers deserve, and that those who oppose the death penalty violate the fundamental principle that criminals should be punished according to their just desserts—"making the punishment fit the crime." If this rule means punishments are unjust unless they are like the crime itself, then the principle is unacceptable: It would require us to rape rapists, torture torturers, and inflict other horrible and degrading punishments on offenders. It would require us to betray traitors and kill multiple murderers again and again—punishments that are, of course, impossible to inflict. Since we cannot reasonably aim to punish all crimes according to this principle, it is arbitrary to invoke it as a requirement of justice in the punishment of murder.

Hugo Adam Bedau, "The Case Against the Death Penalty," http://www.aclu.org/library/case_against_death.html.

Religious Opposition to the Death Penalty

It was the recent highly publicized execution of Karla Faye Tucker, however, that finally put a sympathetic face to the issue of capital punishment and caused many Americans, including religious leaders who have been outspoken advocates of the death penalty, to raise their voices in protest. Tucker's evidently rehabilitated, redeemed, and repentant life illustrated to many for the first time that the death penalty is about nothing more than revenge.

Subsequent executions, including that of another woman, have been met for the most part with a ringing silence from many of those same religious leaders who were so outspoken over Tucker's death. However, for some Christians who traditionally have been supportive of the death penalty, difficult questions have persisted long after the issue left the front pages. For instance, the April 6, 1998, issue of *Christianity Today*, the flagship of mainstream evangelicalism, editorialized against capital punishment for the first time in its history. The *CT* editors wrote, "Jesus' teaching of non-resistance is difficult to live out on a societal level. Not all evangelicals agree on how to apply Jesus' teaching of non-resistance to public policy. But it seems clear that the gospel demands that in ministry, Christians work more for reconciliation than for retribution."

In a political climate that seldom plays to the noblest of our inclinations, "get tough on crime" is a much easier sell than redemption, reconciliation, and rehabilitation. In fact, 84 percent of Americans favor the death penalty under certain circumstances, according to a recent *Newsweek* poll.

Revenge Is Not Justice

Finding justice in the midst of evil can be difficult. Revenge is a much easier emotion to manage. The Catholic archbishop of Denver said recently, "The only true road to justice passes through mercy. Justice cannot be served by more violence." It is increasingly evident that the whole world is watching what we do on this question. Our moral capacity to speak to human rights issues internationally is compromised when we cannot quench our own blood thirst right here at home.

> *"To death penalty opponents in particular, 'an eye for an eye' is a formula for barbarism; . . . Nothing could be more inaccurate."*

Capital Punishment Is Not Vengeful

Jeff Jacoby

Capital punishment is not an act of vengeance, Jeff Jacoby asserts in the following viewpoint. According to Jacoby, death penalty opponents have misinterpreted the Biblical adage "an eye for an eye." He contends that instead of supporting vengeful justice, the "eye for an eye" passage of the Bible is meant to instruct that the guilty must be punished in proportion to their crimes. Jacoby maintains that the Bible overrode the barbarism of earlier days by teaching that punishment must be fair and neither excessive nor lenient. Jacoby is a syndicated columnist.

As you read, consider the following questions:

1. Where in the Bible can the phrase "an eye for an eye" be found, as stated by Jacoby?
2. According to the author, what was the chief concern of ancient lawmakers?
3. What is the average prison sentence for homicide, according to a study cited by Jacoby?

Excerpted from "In Defense of 'An Eye for an Eye,'" by Jeff Jacoby, *Boston Globe*, June 24, 1997. Reprinted with permission from the author.

The jury in Denver votes a death sentence for Timothy McVeigh, and the Page 1 headline in the *Tampa Tribune* declares: "An eye for an eye."

The *Los Angeles Times* editorializes in support of the verdict, triggering an angry reader's protest: "I'm shocked at your editorial. You show yourself to be of the same 'eye for an eye' mindset as McVeigh himself."

Reverend Jesse Jackson says on CBS's "Face the Nation" that McVeigh's crime "makes the toughest case" for opposing the death penalty. But applying the concept of "an eye for an eye," he warns, ultimately "leaves us blind and disfigured."

In Canada, commentator Frank Jones regards the verdict as tragic. "Just for a moment," he laments in the *Toronto Star*, "it seemed people might be ready to turn away from short-sighted eye-for-an-eye vengeance."

Understanding "An Eye for an Eye"

Nothing generates "eye for an eye" references like a death sentence, and the McVeigh verdict has brought them forth in profusion. Sometimes the biblical phrase is used approvingly, as when Donna Hawthorne, the widow of a man murdered in the Oklahoma City bombing, told the *Rocky Mountain News:* "I thought justice was done today—an eye for an eye."

But usually the words are cited pejoratively, as a synechdoche for some "Old Testament" ethic of strict and vengeful justice. To death penalty opponents in particular, "an eye for an eye" is a formula for barbarism; the very phrase suggests a legal system based on mindless and bloody retribution. Nothing could be more inaccurate.

To begin with, they are quoting the wrong phrase. The source of "an eye for an eye" is Exodus 21, the chapter that follows the Ten Commandments. The context is the case of two men in a violent fight, each trying to kill each other. When one man strikes at the second, he misses—and the blow instead wounds a pregnant woman nearby. What is to be done?

That, says Exodus in verses 23-25, depends on how badly she was hurt:

"23. If there shall be a fatality, then you shall award a life for a life.

"24. An eye for an eye, a tooth for a tooth, a hand for a hand, a foot for a foot;

"25. A burn for a burn, a wound for a wound, a bruise for a bruise."

Thus, when the Bible prescribes death for the killer, the term it uses is not "an eye for an eye" but "a life for a life." That is the term that belongs in death penalty discussions and commentary on the McVeigh verdict. "An eye for an eye" is not about capital punishment—it is a stipulation of a lesser punishment for a lesser crime.

The Bible Ushered in Proportionate Justice

A lesser punishment for a lesser crime: What a profound and civilizing principle. To the world in which the Bible first appeared, such a notion—that justice should be proportionate—must have seemed revolutionary. Ancient lawmakers, less concerned with fairness than order, often decreed death for minor offenders, or even innocents. Under the Code of Hammurabi, if Amon built a storehouse for Marduk, and Marduk's daughter died when the building collapsed, Amon's daughter was to be killed in retaliation. How astonishing this new law must have been to the judges of Babylon and Egypt. A legal system under which only the guilty could be punished, and then only in proportion to their crimes? Outlandish!

"An eye for an eye." Not two eyes for an eye, not an eye and a leg for an eye, not your life for an eye. And not just a slap on the wrist either. Exodus teaches a fundamental lesson about justice and decency: Criminal law must not permit vast disparities between the magnitude of the offense and the magnitude of the punishment. It is barbaric to hang pickpockets—as British law was doing not so long ago. It is equally barbaric to turn murderers loose after six or seven years in prison—as American law does today. (According to the U.S. Department of Justice, the average prison sentence served for homicide is five years and 11 months.)

To be sure, "an eye for an eye, a tooth for a tooth" was never taken literally. Jewish law from oldest times interpreted Exodus 21:24-25 as requiring a criminal to pay his victim the monetary equivalent of the blinded eye or broken tooth. (One concern expressed by the rabbis was that putting out a convict's eye could have unintended, perhaps fatal, side effects—thereby increasing his sentence unjustly. But the principle remained: Punishment must be commensurate with the crime, neither cruelly excessive nor unduly lenient.)

PEDRO MEDINA: DIED INSTANTLY IN FLORIDA'S ELECTRIC CHAIR

DOROTHY JAMES: MEDINA'S VICTIM, DIED IN A POOL OF HER OWN BLOOD AN EXCRUCIATING 30 MINUTES AFTER BEING GAGGED AND STABBED 10 TIMES IN THE CHEST

Guess whose death is being labeled 'cruel'?

Cartoon by Mike Thompson. Reprinted by permission of Copley News Service.

For wilfully committing murder, of course, no financial payment could suffice. The one punishment in these verses that was construed literally was "a life for a life." Murder cannot be expiated with money; it is a crime so hideous that only the life of the killer can atone for it. Human blood, Exodus proclaims, is not cheap: This, too, is a notion that ancient rulers—and some not-so-ancient ones—must have found radical and subversive.

It is ironic that the biblical phrase most often cited to denote spiteful vindictiveness stands in fact for exactly the opposite. Fairness, restraint, avoidance of needless cruelty, an insistence on punishing only the guilty—these are the ideas with which "an eye for an eye" enlightened and uplifted human law. Absent that injunction, we would be far less civilized.

| *"It is impossible to undo any penalty imposed on an innocent man."*

Innocent People Could Be Executed

Lester S. Garrett

In the following viewpoint, Lester S. Garrett contends that capital punishment is unjust because innocent people face conviction and possible execution. He presents a variety of cases in which an innocent person was convicted of a crime as a result of false or suppressed evidence. Garrett insists that because these errors and abuses are common, the death penalty must be repealed and replaced with life without parole. Garrett is a Phoenix-based writer.

As you read, consider the following questions:
1. According to the author, how did Fred Zain provide misleading testimony in the Jack Davis trial?
2. How many years did it take to prove Freddie Lee Gains' innocence, as stated by Garrett?
3. In Garrett's view, why do errors and abuse occur in death penalty cases?

Excerpted from "The Executioner's Error," by Lester S. Garrett, *Liberty*, March 1996. Reprinted with permission from *Liberty* magazine.

The same "rigorous" legal procedures and safeguards are applied in each and every capital case. But in some cases brutal killers are sentenced to death; in others, innocent men are sent to the executioner. I repeat: the *same* legal procedures, the *same* jury determination that the defendant is guilty beyond a reasonable doubt, the *same* safeguards, are applied in each case. Yet they send the innocent as well as the guilty to death row.

The Kurt Bloodsworth Case

• In the summer of 1984, a nine-year-old girl was tortured, sodomized, and murdered near her home in Baltimore County, Maryland. Based on circumstantial evidence, 23-year-old Kurt Bloodsworth was convicted and sentenced to death. After two years on death row, Bloodsworth got a new trial on a technicality. Once again he was convicted. This time, however, he received a life sentence.

Nine years later, DNA analysis of the child's garments proved that Bloodsworth could not possibly have been guilty. The wrong man had been sentenced to death.

Unknown to Bloodsworth, three days after his first conviction, police and prosecutors learned about David Rehill. Hours after the girl's murder, Rehill showed up at a mental health clinic with fresh scratches on his face and told one of the therapists that he was "in trouble with a little girl." Rehill resembled the police composite, and, not surprisingly, looked remarkably like Bloodsworth. But Bloodsworth was already behind bars. Six months passed before the police interviewed Rehill. They never bothered to check his alibi or place him in a lineup.

The state had known about Rehill for two years prior to Bloodsworth's second trial. Despite this, that information was withheld from the defense until just days before the trial. His attorneys did not have time to investigate and failed to ask for a postponement. The second jury never learned that there was another potential suspect.

CBS correspondent Edie Magnus reported on the Bloodsworth case for a segment of *Eye To Eye* broadcast October 28, 1993. He asked prosecutor Robert Lazzero to respond "to the criticism that the system closed in on one guy with some evidence, and that everybody just stopped looking at other things that didn't fit."

Lazzero responded, "I would say that, unfortunately, that is not all that rare of an occurrence in our criminal justice system."

Magnus then suggested that the Bloodsworth case demonstrated that "it is eerily easy with a weak case to convict an innocent man."

"Yes," said Lazzero thoughtfully, "in retrospect it is."

An Untrustworthy Medical Examiner

• From 1979 to 1989, Fred Zain was a medical examiner and forensics expert for the West Virginia State Police. During those years, Zain was involved in thousands of criminal cases; his expert testimony was responsible for sending hundreds of defendants to prison.

In 1989, Zain moved to San Antonio, Texas, where he served for the next three years as its crime laboratory's chief serologist. In 1989, Jack Davis was arrested for the sexual assault, murder, and mutilation of Kathie Balonis, a New Braunfels, Texas, woman. At the time, Davis had been employed as a maintenance man at the victim's apartment complex. During Davis' trial, Fred Zain testified that blood specimens found under the victim's body belonged to Davis, who'd cut his hand prior to the murder. There were no eyewitnesses, so Zain's testimony was extremely influential. Davis was convicted of murder and his jury came within a single vote of sentencing him to death.

In 1992, a hearing was convened to investigate prosecutorial misconduct in the Davis case. Davis' defense attorney, Stanley Schneider, explained what had happened: Zain had originally testified that "his testing had proven that blood found under the woman's body came from Davis. Now it comes out that he never did the testing. So Davis was convicted on Zain's lies." Indeed, in a deposition taped about a year later, Zain reversed himself and stated that the blood samples in question actually belonged to the victim and not to Davis. When subsequently questioned under oath about his conflicting statements, Zain refused to answer and invoked his Fifth Amendment protection against self-incrimination.

Judge Charles Ramsey was outraged and said that Zain's conduct was "intentional and outrageous," adding that it "shocked the conscience of the court."

Meanwhile, back in West Virginia, the American Society of Crime Laboratory Directors was investigating Zain's activities there. In November 1993, their report was released. It concluded that Zain "fabricated or falsified evidence in just about every case he touched," including at least 133 murder and rape cases. His actions, stated the report, were the "result of systematic practice rather than an occasional inadvertent error." As a result of that report, the West Virginia Supreme Court ruled, "Any testimony or documentary evidence offered by Zain, at any time, in any criminal prosecution, should be deemed invalid, unreliable and inadmissible."

Zain was dismissed from his Texas job in June of 1993, when evidence vital to the prosecution of a San Antonio murder was lost. Subsequently, Bexar County Medical Examiner Vincent DiMaio hired Irving Stone of the Institute of Forensic Science in Dallas to conduct an extensive review of Zain's work during his period of employment in San Antonio. According to the *San Francisco Examiner*, Stone's team discovered "reports from tests that were never done, negative results that would have cleared a suspect reported as positive and inconclusive results described as conclusive." Said Stone: "Everything that Fred Zain did, whether it was in West Virginia or Texas, has to be suspect, and it worries me to the point that [the tests] ought to be repeated." Estimates of the total number of cases in which Zain was involved vary from 1,200 to 4,500 (the latter is Stone's).

More Miscarriages of Justice

• In August of 1980, Clarence Lee Brandley, a black janitorial supervisor for a Conroe, Texas, school, was convicted of rape and sentenced to death. Evidence that would have exonerated him had been deliberately suppressed. He received his first stay five days from his scheduled execution. His second stay was granted 13 days from his final walk. Brandley spent nine and a half years in [jail] while appealing his conviction. It was finally overturned in 1989, and Brandley was released in January of 1990.

• And then there's the case of Randall Dale Adams, made famous by the film *The Thin Blue Line*. Adams was found guilty beyond a reasonable doubt of killing a police officer. Sentenced to death, his appeals were rejected. Just 72 hours from execution, by a stroke of good fortune, he was granted a stay of execution. It was soon established that the wrong man was about to be put to death, and Adams was released.

The strongest argument against capital punishment

Reprinted by permission of Ann Telnaes.

• It took 13 years to prove that Freddie Lee Gains was not guilty of murder. Thirteen years before an innocent man was freed. Keep that in mind the next time you hear someone demand that we shorten the appeals process. Years after Gains' trial, conviction, and death sentence in Birmingham, Alabama, one of the actual perpetrators, who was arrested for another crime in Florida, confessed. Gains, who had insisted all along that he was innocent, would be dead now if the advocates of shortening the appeals process had had their way.

• In August of 1978, Matthew Conner was convicted of the rape, murder, and brutal mutilation of a twelve-year-old girl. He spent twelve years in prison before boxes of concealed evidence were discovered in the possession of the district attorney—evidence that, had it not been denied his lawyer at the time of his trial, would have established that he was not guilty.

• In California, Benny Powell and Clarence Chance were convicted for the murder of a sheriff's deputy. In 1992, after spending 17 years in prison, they were released, after the Los Angeles district attorney admitted that the two black men had been wrongfully convicted and joined with their defense attorney in a motion for their release.

It must be stressed that all these men were subjected to the exact same procedure as the Ted Bundys. They too were found guilty beyond a reasonable doubt. But *they* were innocent. They are not someone's hypotheticals; they are real, flesh-and-blood human beings who were wrongly convicted and sentenced to death. And lest I be misunderstood, let me make it clear that I have no compassion whatsoever for brutal killers. It is myself, my family, and my friends who concern me—as they should you.

Eliminate the Death Penalty

The state can never give back to Benny Powell and Clarence Chance the 17 years they spent in prison for a crime they didn't commit. It is impossible to undo any penalty imposed on an innocent man. But it is possible to mitigate that penalty, to give victims like Powell and Chance back the remainder of their natural lives. There is no way to give a man back his life should you discover that a horrible mistake has been made.

The potential for error and abuse is, of necessity, inherent in the system. As the stories above make all too clear, this is not some vague, hypothetical theory. It is all too frighteningly real. Shorten the appeals process, and many of those innocent men would long since have been executed. (One wonders: How many innocent victims have been executed over the years who would have been exonerated had they been allowed a longer appeal process?)

We must repeal the death penalty and substitute life without parole for *our* own protection. Not against some long-past abuse, but against the abuse and error that occurs today and will occur tomorrow and for as long as human beings administer a criminal justice system. It is to protect each and every one of us from racial prejudice, from ambitious prosecutors who have forgotten why they are there, from incompetent defense attorneys, and from *innocent error.* We must never forget that prosecutors, judges, expert witnesses, and jurors are no more immune to prejudice, blind ambition, or error than the rest of us. The death penalty allows the state to bury its mistakes, leaving the guilty to walk free. Once an innocent man is executed, no one is likely to continue investigating his case.

If we truly believe in justice, we must abolish the death penalty.

"There is, . . . no proof that an innocent has been executed since 1900."

Innocent People Have Not Been Executed

Justice for All

Justice for All is a not-for-profit organization whose members believe that the criminal justice system does not adequately protect law-abiding citizens. The organization asserts in the following viewpoint that, despite the claims of some anti-capital punishment activists, there is no evidence that innocent people have been executed under America's death penalty laws. The organization claims that certain studies, which suggest that numerous people on death row are innocent, are riddled with flaws. According to Justice for All, errors in death penalty cases are extremely rare, if they exist at all.

As you read, consider the following questions:

1. What percentage of death penalty cases has been overturned since 1973, according to Justice for All?
2. According to the organization, what are the flaws in the Bedau-Radelet study?
3. What is fraudulent about the James Adams report, in the organization's view?

Excerpted from "Death Penalty and Sentencing Information in the United States," by Justice for All, October 1, 1997, found at www.prodeathpenalty.com/DP.html. Reprinted with permission.

Great effort has been made in pretrial, trial, appeals, writ and clemency procedures to minimize the chance of an innocent [person] being convicted, sentenced to death or executed. Since 1973, legal protections have been so extraordinary that 37% of all death row cases have been overturned for due process reasons or commuted. Indeed, inmates are six times more likely to get off death row by appeals than by execution. And, in fact, many of those cases were overturned based on post conviction new laws, established by legislative or judicial decisions in other cases.

Opponents claim that 69 "innocent" death row inmates have been released since 1973. Just a casual review, using the Death Penalty Information Center's (DPIC's) own case descriptions, reveals that of 39 cases reviewed, that the DPIC offers no evidence of innocence in 29, or 78%, of those cases. Incredibly, the DPIC reviews "Recent Cases of Possible Mistaken Executions," wherein they list the cases of Roger Keith Coleman, Leonel Herrera, and Jesse Jacobs—3 cases which helped solidify the anti-death penalty movement penchant for lack of full disclosure and/or fraud. For the fourth case, therein, that of Coleman Wayne Gray, the DPIC makes no effort to claim innocence.

Furthermore, the DPIC and most opponents fail to review that the role of clemency and appeals in such cases is to judge the merits of death row inmates claims regarding innocence and/or additional trial error. Indeed, the release of those 69 inmates proves that such procedures worked precisely, and often generously, as intended. Also contrary to opponents' claims, clemency is used generously to grant mercy to death row murderers and to spare inmates whose guilt has come into question. In fact, 135 death row inmates have been spared by clemency or commutation from 1973-95. This represents 43% of the total of those executed during that time—a remarkable record of consideration and mercy.

In reviewing the DPIC's original 1993 study, finding 48 (of the 69) "innocent" defendants on death row, the DPIC states its debt for the " . . . groundbreaking work done by . . . Professors Michael Radelet and Hugo Bedau" in their "Miscarriages of Justice in Potentially Capital Cases."

The most significant study conducted to evaluate the evidence of the "innocent executed" is the Bedau-Radelet Study ("Miscarriages of Justice in Potentially Capital Cases," 40, 1 Stanford Law Review, 11/87). The study concluded that 23 innocent persons had been executed since 1900. However, the study's methodology was so flawed that at least 12 of those cases had no evidence of innocence and substantial evidence of guilt. Bedau & Radelet, both opponents, "consistently presented incomplete and misleading accounts of the evidence." (Markman, Stephen J. & Cassell, Paul G., "Protecting the Innocent: A Response to the Bedau-Radelet Study" 41, 1 Stanford Law Review, 11/88). The remaining 11 cases represent 0.14% of the 7,800 executions which have taken place since 1900. And, there is, in fact, no proof that those 11 executed were innocent. In addition, the "innocents executed" group was extracted from a Bedau & Radelet imagined pool of 350 persons who were, supposedly, wrongly convicted of capital or "potentially" capital crimes. Not only were they at least 50% in error with their 23 "innocents executed" claim, but 211 of those 350 cases, or 60%, were not sentenced to death. Bedau and Radelet already knew that plea bargains, the juries, the evidence, the prosecutors, judicial review and/or the legal statutes had put these crimes in the "no capital punishment" category. Indeed, their claims of innocence, regarding the remaining 139 of those 350 cases, should be suspect, given this study's poor level of accuracy. Calling their work misleading hardly does this "academic" study justice. Had a high school student presented such a report, where 50–60% of the material was either false or misleading, a grade of F would be a likely result.

Indeed, Michigan Court of Appeals Judge Stephen Markman finds that " . . . the Bedau-Radelet study is remarkable not (as retired Supreme Court Judge Harry Blackmun seems to believe) for demonstrating that mistakes involving the death penalty are common, but rather for demonstrating how uncommon they are . . . This study—the most thorough and painstaking analysis ever on the subject—fails to prove that a single such mistake has occurred in the United States during the twentieth century." Presumably, Bedau and Radelet would have selected the most compelling 23 cases of the innocent executed to prove their proposition. "Yet, in each of these cases, where there is a record to review, there are eye-witnesses, confessions, physical evidence and circumstantial evidence in support of the defendant's guilt. Bedau has written elsewhere that it is 'false sentimentality to argue that the death penalty ought to be abolished because of the abstract possibility that an innocent person might be executed when the record fails to disclose that such cases exist.' . . . (T)he Bedau and Radelet study . . . speaks eloquently about the extraordinary rarity of error in capital punishment."

Another significant oversight by that study was not differentiating between the risk of executing innocent persons before and after *Furman v. Georgia* (1972). There is, in fact, no proof that an innocent has been executed since 1900. And the probability of such a tragedy occurring has been lowered significantly more since *Furman*. In the context that hundreds of thousands of innocents have been murdered or seriously injured, since 1900, by criminals improperly released by the U.S. criminal justice system (or not incarcerated at all!), the relevant question is: Is the risk of executing the innocent, however slight, worth the justifications for the death penalty—those being retribution, rehabilitation, incapacitation, required punishment, deterrence, escalating punishments, religious mandates, cost savings, the moral imperative, just punishment and the saving of innocent lives?

Fraudulent Claims

Predictably, opponents still continue to fraudulently claim, even today, that this study has proven that 23 "innocent" people have been executed, even though Bedau and Radelet, the authors of that study, conceded—in 1988—that neither they nor any previous researchers have proved that any of those executed was innocent: "We agree with our critics that we have not proved these executed defendants to be innocent; we never claimed that we had."

One of opponents' most blatant frauds is their claim that the U.S. Supreme Court, in [the 1993 case] *Herrera v. Collins*, found that the Herrera "decision would allow the states to execute a defendant for a crime that he did not commit. Justice O'Connor's concurring opinion makes clear that Herrera does not stand for that proposition. Justice O'Connor stated,

'I cannot disagree with the fundamental legal principal that executing the innocent is inconsistent with the Constitution' and 'the execution of a legally and factually innocent person would be a constitutionally intolerable event.' As Justice O'-Connor stated, the Court assumed for the sake of argument 'that a truly persuasive demonstration of actual innocence would render any such execution unconstitutional and that federal habeas relief would be warranted if no state avenue were open to process the claim.' That is the holding in Herrera, and any claim to the contrary is simply not correct."

Errors Do Not Negate the Death Penalty

Society has a right to protect itself from capital offenses even if this means taking a finite chance of executing an innocent person. If the basic activity or process is justified, then it is regrettable, but morally acceptable, that some mistakes are made. Fire trucks occasionally kill innocent pedestrians while racing to fires, but we accept these losses as justified by the greater good of the activity of using fire trucks. We judge the use of automobiles to be acceptable even though such use causes an average of 50,000 traffic fatalities each year. We accept the morality of a defensive war even though it will result in our troops accidentally or mistakenly killing innocent people.

The fact that we can err in applying the death penalty should give us pause and cause us to build an appeals process into the judicial system. Such a process is already in the American and British legal systems. That occasional error may be made, regrettable though this is, is not a sufficient reason for us to refuse to use the death penalty, if on balance it serves a just and useful function.

Louis P. Pojman and Jeffrey Reiman, *The Death Penalty: For and Against*, 1998.

"Moreover, Herrera's claim of innocence was weak at best, seeking to blame his dead brother for the crimes Herrera was found guilty of committing. When the evidence against Herrera is considered against the proffered evidence of innocence, it is not surprising that none of the federal judges to hear this claim, including the dissenters in the Supreme Court, have ever expressed any doubt as to Herrera's guilt." (Kenneth S. Nunnelley in Congressional testimony, July 23, 1993.)

Dishonesty in the James Adams Report

Stephen Bright, Director, Southern Center For Human Rights (Atlanta, Ga.) claims that Aubrey Adams of Florida represents a case of the "innocent" executed. Since neither Justice for All (JFA) nor the Death Penalty Information Center could locate an Aubrey Adams for which such claims had been made, JFA assumes that Mr. Bright meant the well known case of James Adams of Florida.

The James Adams case is particularly worthy of review. Not only is the Adams case one of those alleged 23 "innocent" executed, but his is the only post-*Furman* case cited by Bedau and Radelet. Bedau and Radelet's claims and "evidence" are too lengthy to review here. A short review is all that is required to discredit such claims. They "proved" Adams' innocence by a review, not of the case facts, but of Adams' own claims from his clemency hearing! This dishonest review was presented as an objective evaluation of the case when, in fact, it was completely biased, with only one goal—to present the case facts in the light most favorable to Adams and to neglect or suppress the voluminous evidence of Adams' guilt. Cassell and Markman exposed this academic fraud and presented the case facts from the full record, as Bedau and Radelet should have. The case for Adams' guilt is solid. . . .

Both Bedau and Radelet refused to claim that Adams was innocent. Yet, this does not prevent opponents from making false claims to the contrary. If Mr. Bright was discussing the James Adams case, this is a classic, standard example of the type of anti–death penalty fraud found every day.

Irresponsible editors, publishers and authors are common within this debate. Two examples: *Punishment and the Death Penalty*, Baird, Robert & Rosenbaum, Stuart, Prometheus, 1996 and *Capital Punishment: The Death Penalty Debate*, Gottfried, Ted, Enslow, 1997. Both still claim that 23 "innocents" have been executed!

Periodical Bibliography

The following articles have been selected to supplement the diverse views presented in this chapter. Addresses are provided for periodicals not indexed in the *Readers' Guide to Periodical Literature*, the *Alternative Press Index*, the *Social Sciences Index*, or the *Index to Legal Periodicals and Books*.

Craig Aaron	"Criminal Injustice System," *In These Times*, December 27, 1998.
Pat Buchanan	"Death Penalty Is Act of Retribution, Not Revenge," *Conservative Chronicle*, February 18, 1998. Available from PO Box 29, Hampton, IA 50441.
William F. Buckley Jr.	"Miss Tucker's Plea," *National Review*, March 9, 1998.
Robert E. Burns	"Pull the Plug on the Death Penalty," *U.S. Catholic*, August 1998.
Fox Butterfield	"Ambivalence? Incompetence? Fairness?: Behind the Death Row Bottleneck," *New York Times*, December 25, 1998.
Fox Butterfield	"New Study Adds to Evidence of Bias in Death Sentences," *New York Times*, June 7, 1998.
Charles Chaput, Arthur Tafoya, and Richard Hanifen	"Once-in-a-Generation Crossroad: Capital Punishment," *Origins*, October 23, 1997. Available from Catholic News Service, 3211 4th St. NE, Washington, DC 20017-1100.
David Gelernter	"What Do Murderers Deserve?" *Commentary*, April 1998.
Judy Gross	"Executions Continue; So Does Debate," *National Catholic Reporter*, February 20, 1998. Available from 115 East Armour Blvd., Kansas City, MO 64111.
Issues and Controversies On File	"Death Penalty," May 1, 1998. Available from Facts On File News Services, 11 Penn Plaza, New York, NY 10001-2006.
Marlene Martin	"The Politics of the Death Penalty," *International Socialist Review*, Winter 1997.
John McCormick	"The Wrongly Condemned," *Newsweek*, November 9, 1998.
Helen Prejean	"Walking Through the Fire," *The Other Side*, September-December 1997.

Tony Snow   "Some Crimes Deserve Capital Punishment," *Conservative Chronicle*, June 18, 1997.

Wall Street Journal   "Gender and Death," February 2, 1998.

Marvin E. Wolfgang   "We Do Not Deserve to Kill," *Crime & Delinquency*, January 1998. Available from Sage Publications, 2455 Teller Rd., Thousand Oaks, CA 91320.

For Further Discussion

Chapter 1

1. Ernest van den Haag argues that suicide can be a moral choice. He believes that society has no good reason to prohibit mentally competent people from committing suicide, and that it has traditionally been stigmatized only because of taboos about death. Do you agree with van den Haag's contention that suicide should be destigmatized? Why does Daniel Callahan believe that most societies have traditionally frowned on suicide? Do you think his reasons justify the prohibition of suicide? Explain your answers.

2. Margaret Pabst Battin considers several classical arguments condemning suicide. Which of these classical arguments do you find most persuasive, and why? Do you feel that Battin adequately refutes the argument you've chosen? Why or why not?

Chapter 2

1. Andrew Bernstein argues that since individuals have a right to control their own bodies, they have a right to suicide. Peter J. Bernardi argues that an individual has obligations to society that sometimes outweigh individual rights. Do you feel that individuals have a right to commit suicide if they choose? Why or why not? Now consider physician-assisted suicide: Do you believe individuals have a right to a physician's assistance in committing suicide? In what ways are the two proposed rights different?

2. Joram Graf Haber proposes that physician-assisted suicide be tolerated by society as a "poorly kept secret," in much the same way that driving a little above the speed limit is technically illegal but often ignored. Given the American Foundation for Suicide Prevention's claim that assisted suicide and euthanasia are abused in the Netherlands, what objections would the AFSP have to Haber's proposal? Also consider Faye Girsh's argument that legalization of assisted suicide would help reduce abuse of the practice—do you think she would endorse Haber's approach? What is your own opinion of tolerating, but not legalizing, physician-assisted suicide?

3. Both R. Henry Capps Jr. and the American Foundation of Suicide Prevention contend that patients who want to die should be given psychological treatment for depression and palliative or hospice care for pain relief. How does Joram Graf Haber re-

spond to the argument that a desire to die must be motivated by depression, and therefore irrational? How does Faye Girsh respond to the argument that hospice and palliative care can alleviate the need for physician-assisted suicide? In each case, whose arguments are most convincing, and why?

Chapter 3

1. John M. Swomley is an emeritus professor at a school of theology. Heather King has had three abortions. Given their life histories, do you find the conclusions they reached concerning the ethics of abortion surprising? Why or why not?

2. After reading the viewpoints by Ann Bradley and Gregg L. Cunningham, do you think that aborting handicapped fetuses is an ethical decision or one that could lead to the justification of infanticide and euthanasia? Explain your answer.

3. Marilyn French argues that the right to abortion gives women more control over their bodies, while Carolyn C. Gargaro contends that abortion rights provide greater freedom to men. Whose argument do you find more convincing and why?

Chapter 4

1. After reading the viewpoints in this chapter, do you believe that capital punishment is just, or that it should be replaced by a sentence of life without parole? Explain your answer.

2. Jeff Jacoby focuses his argument justifying capital punishment on the Biblical teaching "an eye for an eye." Do you believe that this adage, written several thousand years ago, is relevant to the modern justice system? Why or why not?

3. Although Lester S. Garrett does not name any innocent person who was executed, he details several cases in which a wrongfully convicted person was spared from death, sometimes only a few days before the scheduled execution. Justice for All contends that no innocent prisoner has ever been executed and that such a situation is unlikely to occur. Which viewpoint do you find more convincing and why?

Organizations to Contact

The editors have compiled the following list of organizations concerned with the issues debated in this book. The descriptions are derived from materials provided by the organizations. All have publications or information available for interested readers. The list was compiled on the date of publication of the present volume; the information provided here may change. Be aware that many organizations take several weeks or longer to respond to inquiries, so allow as much time as possible.

American Association of Suicidology (AAS)
4201 Connecticut Ave. NW, Suite 408, Washington, DC 20008
(202) 237-2280 • fax: (202) 237-2282
e-mail: debbiehu@ix.netcom.com
website: http://www.suicidology.org
The association is one of the largest suicide prevention organizations in the United States. It promotes the view that suicidal thoughts are almost always a symptom of depression and that suicide is almost never a rational decision. In addition to prevention of suicide, the group also works to increase public awareness about suicide and to help those grieving the death of a loved one to suicide. The association publishes the quarterly newsletters *American Association of Suicidology—Newslink* and *Surviving Suicide*, and the quarterly journal *Suicide and Life Threatening Behavior.*

Amnesty International USA (AI)
322 Eighth Ave., New York, NY 10001
(212) 807-8400 • fax: (212) 627-1451
website: http://www.amnesty-usa.org
Amnesty International is an independent worldwide movement working impartially for the release of all prisoners of conscience, fair and prompt trials for political prisoners, and an end to torture and executions. AI is funded by donations from its members and supporters throughout the world. AI has published several books and reports, including *Fatal Flaws: Innocence and the Death Penalty.*

American Foundation for Suicide Prevention (AFSP)
120 Wall Street, 22nd Floor, New York, NY 10005
(888) 333-2377 • fax: (212) 363-6237
e-mail: rfabrika@afsp.org • website: http://www.afsp.org
Formerly known as the American Suicide Foundation, the AFSP supports scientific research on depression and suicide, educates the public and professionals on the recognition and treatment of depressed and suicidal individuals, and provides support programs for

those coping with the loss of a loved one to suicide. It opposes the legalization of physician-assisted suicide. AFSP publishes a policy statement on physician-assisted suicide, the newsletter *Crisis*, and the quarterly *Lifesavers*.

American Life League (ALL)
PO Box 1350, Stafford, VA 22555
(540) 659-4171 • fax: (540) 659-2586
e-mail: whylife@all.org • website: http://www.all.org

ALL is an educational pro-life organization that opposes abortion, artificial contraception, reproductive technologies, and fetal experimentation. It asserts that it is immoral to perform experiments on living human embryos and fetuses. ALL works to educate Americans about the dangers of all forms of euthanasia and opposes legislative efforts that would legalize or increase its incidence. It publishes the bimonthly pro-life magazine *Celebrate Life*, and distributes videos, brochures, and newsletters monitoring euthanasia-related developments.

Canadian Coalition Against the Death Penalty (CCADP)
80 Lillington Ave., Toronto, ON, M1N 3K7 Canada
(416) 693-9112 • fax: (416) 686-1630
e-mail: ccadp@home.com • website: http://www.ccadp.org

CCADP is a not-for-profit international human rights organization dedicated to educating on alternatives to the death penalty worldwide and to providing emotional and practical support to death row inmates, their families, and the families of murder victims. The center releases pamphlets and periodic press releases, and its website includes a student resource center providing research information on capital punishment.

Catholics for a Free Choice (CFFC)
1436 U St. NW, Suite 301, Washington, DC 20009-3997
(202) 986-6093 • fax: (202) 332-7995
website: http://www.cath4choice.org

CFFC supports the right to legal abortion and promotes family planning to reduce the incidence of abortion and to increase women's choice in childbearing and child rearing. It publishes the bimonthly newsletter *Conscience*, the booklet *The History of Abortion in the Catholic Church*, and the brochure *You Are Not Alone*.

Death with Dignity
1818 N St. NW, Suite 450, Washington, DC 20036
(202) 530-2900
e-mail: info@deathwithdignity.org
website: http://www.deathwithdignity.org

Death with Dignity promotes a comprehensive, humane, responsive system of care for terminally ill patients. Its members believe that a dying patient's choices should be given the utmost respect and consideration. The center serves as an information resource for the public and the media and promotes strategies for advancing a responsive system of care for terminally ill patients on educational, legal, legislative, and public-policy fronts. It publishes several fact sheets, including *Misconceptions in the Debate on Death with Dignity*, *The Situation in Florida*, *Dying in the U.S.A.: A Call for Public Debate*, and *The Issue: From the Individual's Perspective*, all of which are available in an information package by request.

Feminists for Life of America
733 15th St. NW, Suite 1100, Washington, DC 20005
(202) 737-3352
e-mail: fems4life@aol.com • website: www.feministsforlife.org

This organization is comprised of individuals united to secure the right to life, from conception to natural death, for all human beings. It believes that legal abortion exploits women. The group supports a Human Life Amendment, the Equal Rights Amendment, and other methods it believes will achieve respect for life and equality. Publications include the quarterly *Sisterlife*, the book *Prolife Feminism: Different Voices*, the booklet *Early Feminist Case Against Abortion*, and the pamphlet *Abortion Does Not Liberate Women*.

The Hemlock Society
PO Box 101810, Denver, CO 80250
(800) 247-7421 • (303) 639-1202 • fax: (303) 639-1224
e-mail: hemlock@privatei.com
website: http://www.hemlock.org

The society believes that terminally ill individuals have the right to commit suicide. The society publishes books on suicide, death, and dying, including *Final Exit*, a guide for those suffering with terminal illnesses and considering suicide. The Hemlock Society also publishes the newsletter *TimeLines*.

Human Life International (HLI)
4 Family Life Lane, Front Royal, VA 22630
(540) 635-7884 • fax: (540) 635-7363
e-mail: hli@hli.org • website: http://www.hli.org

HLI categorically rejects abortion and euthanasia and believes assisted suicide is morally unacceptable. It defends the rights of the unborn, the disabled, and those threatened by euthanasia, and it provides education, advocacy, and support services. HLI publishes the monthly newsletters *HLI Reports*, *HLI Update*, and *Deacons Circle*.

International Anti-Euthanasia Task Force (IAETF)
PO Box 760, Steubenville, OH 43952
(740) 282-3810
e-mail: info@iaetf.org • website: http://www.iaetf.org
The task force opposes euthanasia, assisted suicide, and policies that threaten the lives of the medically vulnerable. IAETF publishes fact sheets and position papers on euthanasia-related topics in addition to the bimonthly newsletter, *IAETF Update*. It analyzes the policies and legislation concerning medical and social work organizations and files *amicus curaie* briefs in major "right-to-die" cases.

Justice for All (JFA)
PO Box 55159, Houston, TX 77255
(713) 935-9300 • fax: (713) 935-9301
e-mail: jfanet@msn.com • website: http://www.jfa.net
Justice for All is a not-for-profit criminal justice reform organization that supports the death penalty. Its activities include circulating online petitions to keep violent offenders from being paroled early and publishing the monthly newsletter *The Voice of Justice*.

Lincoln Institute for Research and Education
1001 Connecticut Ave. NW, Washington, DC 20036
(202) 223-5112
The institute is a conservative think tank that studies public policy issues affecting the lives of black Americans, including the issue of the death penalty, which it favors. It publishes the quarterly *Lincoln Review.*

National Abortion and Reproductive Rights Action League (NARAL)
1156 15th St. NW, Suite 700, Washington, DC 20005
(202) 973-3000 • fax: (202) 973-3096
e-mail: naral@naral.org • website: http://www.naral.org
NARAL works to develop and sustain a pro-choice political constituency in order to maintain the right of all women to legal abortion. The league briefs members of Congress and testifies at hearings on abortion and related issues. It publishes the quarterly *NARAL Newsletter.*

National Hospice Organization (NHO)
1700 Diagonal Rd., Suite 300, Alexandria, VA 22314
(800) 658-8898 • (703) 243-5900 • fax: (703) 525-5762
e-mail: drsnho@cais.org • website: http://www.nho.org
The organization works to educate the public about the benefits of hospice care for the terminally ill and their families. It seeks to pro-

mote the idea that with the proper care and pain medication, the terminally ill can live out their lives comfortably and in the company of their families. It publishes the quarterlies *Hospice Journal* and *Hospice Magazine*, as well as books and monographs.

National Coalition to Abolish the Death Penalty (NCADP)
1436 U St. NW, Suite 104, Washington, DC 20009
(202) 387-3890 • fax: (202) 387-5590
e-mail: info@ncadp • website: http://www.ncadp.org
The National Coalition to Abolish the Death Penalty is a collection of more than 115 groups working together to stop executions in the United States. The organization compiles statistics on the death penalty. To further its goal, the coalition publishes *Legislative Action to Abolish the Death Penalty*, information packets, pamphlets, and research materials.

National Right to Life Committee (NRLC)
419 7th St. NW, Suite 500, Washington, DC 20004
(202) 626-8800
e-mail: nrlc@nrlc.org • website: http://www.nrlc.org
NRLC is one of the largest organizations opposing abortion. The committee campaigns against legislation to legalize abortion. It encourages ratification of a constitutional amendment granting embryos and fetuses the same right to life as living persons, and it advocates alternatives to abortion, such as adoption. NRLC publishes the brochure *When Does Life Begin?* and the periodic tabloid *National Right to Life News*.

Planned Parenthood Federation of America (PPFA)
810 Seventh Ave., New York, NY 10019
(212) 541-7800 • fax: (212) 245-1845
e-mail: communictions@ppfa.org • website: http://www.planned-parenthood.org
PPFA is a national organization that supports people's right to make their own reproductive decisions without governmental interference. It provides contraception, abortion, and family planning services at clinics located throughout the United States. Among its extensive publications are the pamphlets *Abortions: Questions and Answers, Five Ways to Prevent Abortion,* and *Nine Reasons Why Abortions Are Legal.*

Bibliography of Books

James R. Acker, Robert M. Bohm, and Charles S. Lanier, eds. — *America's Experiment with Capital Punishment: Reflections on the Past, Present, and Future of the Ultimate Penal Sanction.* Durham, NC: Carolina Academic Press, 1998.

Amnesty International — *United States of America: "A Macabre Assembly Line of Death"—Death Penalty Developments in 1997.* New York: Amnesty International USA Publications, 1998.

Margaret P. Battin — *The Death Debate: Ethical Issues in Suicide.* Upper Saddle River, NJ: Prentice-Hall, 1996.

Margaret P. Battin, Rosamond Rhodes, and Anita Silvers, eds. — *Physician-Assisted Suicide: Expanding the Debate.* New York: Routledge, 1998.

Hugo Adam Bedau, ed. — *The Death Penalty in America.* New York: Oxford University Press, 1997.

John D. Bessler — *Death in the Dark: Midnight Executions in America.* Boston: Northeastern University Press, 1997.

Mary Boyle — *Re-Thinking Abortion: Psychology, Gender, Power, and the Law.* London: Routledge, 1997.

Ira Byock — *Dying Well: Peace and Possibilities at the End of Life.* New York: Riverhead Books, 1997.

Committee on Medical Ethics, Episcopal Diocese of Washington, DC — *Assisted Suicide and Euthanasia: Christian Moral Perspectives: The Washington Report.* Harrisburg, PA: Morehouse, 1997.

Kimberly J. Cook — *Divided Passions: Public Opinions on Abortion and the Death Penalty.* Boston: Northeastern University Press, 1998.

Victor Cosculluela — *The Ethics of Suicide.* New York: Garland, 1995.

Mark Costanzo — *Just Revenge: Costs and Consequences of the Death Penalty.* New York: St. Martin's Press, 1997.

Timothy J. Demy and Gary P. Stewart, eds. — *Suicide: A Christian Response: Crucial Considerations for Choosing Life.* Grand Rapids, MI: Kregel, 1998.

Susan Dwyer and Joel Feinberg, eds. — *The Problem of Abortion.* Belmont, CA: Wadsworth Publishing, 1997.

Linda L. Emanuel, ed. — *Regulating How We Die: The Ethical, Medical, and Legal Issues Surrounding Physician-Assisted Suicide.* Cambridge, MA: Harvard University Press, 1998.

| Sally B. Geis, ed. | *How Shall We Die?: Helping Christians Debate Assisted Suicide*. Nashville, TN: Abingdon Press, 1997. |

Herbert H. Haines — *Against Capital Punishment: The Anti-Death Penalty Movement in America, 1972–1994*. New York: Oxford University Press, 1996.

Herbert Hendin — *Seduced by Death: Doctors, Patients, and the Dutch Cure*. New York: W.W. Norton, 1998.

Herbert Hendin — *Suicide in America*. New York: W.W. Norton, 1995.

Burt Henson and Ross R. Olney — *Furman v. Georgia: The Constitution and the Death Penalty*. New York: Franklin Watts, 1996.

Derek Humphry and Mary Clement — *Freedom to Die: People, Politics, and the Right-to-Die Movement*. New York: St. Martin's Press, 1998.

Kay R. Jamison — *Night Falls Fast: Understanding Suicide*. New York: Knopf, 1999.

Stephen Jamison — *Final Acts of Love: Families, Friends, and Assisted Dying*. New York: J.P. Tarcher, 1995.

John Keown, ed. — *Euthanasia Examined: Ethical, Clinical and Legal Perspectives*. New York: Cambridge University Press, 1995.

Patrick Lee — *Abortion and Unborn Human Life*. Washington, DC: Catholic University of America Press, 1996.

Michael Manning — *Euthanasia and Physician-Assisted Suicide: Killing or Caring?* Mahwah, NJ: Paulist Press, 1998.

Eric Marcus — *Why Suicide?: Answers to 200 of the Most Frequently Asked Questions About Suicide, Attempted Suicide, and Assisted Suicide*. San Francisco: Harper, 1996.

Eileen L. McDonagh — *Breaking the Abortion Deadlock: From Choice to Consent*. New York: Oxford University Press, 1996.

Michael Mello — *Dead Wrong: A Death Row Lawyer Speaks Out Against Capital Punishment*. Madison: University of Wisconsin Press, 1997.

Jonathan D. Moreno — *Arguing Euthanasia: The Controversy over Mercy Killing*. New York: Simon & Schuster, 1995.

Louis P. Pojman and Jeffrey Reiman — *The Death Penalty: For and Against*. Lanham, MD: Rowman & Littlefield, 1998.

Suzanne T. Poppema with Mike Henderson — *Why I Am an Abortion Doctor*. Amherst, NY: Prometheus Books, 1996.

James Risen and   *Wrath of Angels: The American Abortion War.*
Judy L. Thomas   New York: BasicBooks, 1998.

William Schabas   *The Death Penalty As Cruel Treatment and Tor-
                      ture: Capital Punishment Challenged in the World's
                      Courts.* Boston: Northeastern University Press,
                      1996.

Wesley J. Smith   *Forced Exit: The Slippery Slope from Assisted Sui-
                      cide to Legalized Murder.* New York: Times
                      Books, 1997.

Rickie Solinger, ed. *Abortion Wars: A Half Century of Struggle, 1950-
                      2000.* Berkeley: University of California Press,
                      1998.

Lloyd Steffen   *Executing Justice: The Moral Meaning of the
                      Death Penalty.* Cleveland: Pilgrim Press, 1998.

Raymond Tatalovich   *The Politics of Abortion in the United States and
                      Canada: A Comparative Study.* Armonk, NY:
                      M.E. Sharpe, 1997.

Michael Thomson   *Reproducing Narrative: Gender, Reproduction, and
                      Law.* Brookfield, VT: Ashgate, 1998.

Michael M. Uhlmann,   *Last Rights?: Assisted Suicide and Euthanasia
ed.   Debated.* Grand Rapids, MI: William B. Eerd-
                      mans, 1998.

Robert F. Weir   *Ethical Issues in Suicide.* Upper Saddle River, NJ:
                      Prentice-Hall, 1995.

Robert F. Weir, ed.   *Physician-Assisted Suicide.* Bloomington: Indiana
                      University Press, 1997.

James L. Werth, ed.   *Contemporary Perspectives on Rational Suicide.*
                      Levittown, PA: Brunner/Mazel, 1998.

Kevin Wm. Wildes and *Choosing Life: A Dialogue on Evangelium Vitae.*
Alan C. Mitchell, eds. Washington, DC: Georgetown University
                      Press, 1997.

Index

premature babies, 121, 125
Press Democrat (newspaper), 62
Principles of Anesthesiology (Collins), 124
pro-choice movement, 13, 104, 108
  on aborting handicapped fetuses, 114
  on assault-induced pregnancy, 98
  wants abortion on request, 118
prolepsis, 103
pro-life feminists
  reject use of violence, 134
  respect all human life, 133, 134, 135, 136
  want real choices for women, 133–34
pro-life movement, 12–13, 14, 100–102, 103–104, 108
  on assault-induced pregnancy, 98
  on fetal handicaps, 114, 117
  and living children, 129
  on miscarriages, 101–102
  urges adoption, 103
  uses propaganda, 103
Ptolemy II, 41
Punishment and the Death Penalty (Baird and Rosenbaum), 171
Purrington, Sue, 133

Quakers, 102
Quill, Timothy E., 69

Radelet, Michael, 167
Ramsey, Charles, 162
rape, 98, 131, 133
Reardon, David C., 98
Rehill, David, 160
Reiman, Jeffrey, 170
religious leaders
  on abortion, 101–102
  on the death penalty, 139, 153–54
  on physician-assisted suicide, 57, 84–85
Remmelink Report, 92
Reporter Dispatch (newspaper), 103
reproductive technology, 115
right-to-die movement, 53, 56–58, 60, 77, 83
  overlooks advances in palliative care, 74
Robertson, Pat, 139
Robert Woods Johnson Foundation, 84
Rocky Mountain News (newspaper), 156
Roe v. Wade, 12, 61
Rosenbaum, Stuart, 171
Rothman, Barbara Katz, 115
Royal College of Obstetricians and Gynaecologists, 115
Rwandans, 152

Saint Louis Post Dispatch (newspaper), 147

San Francisco Examiner (newspaper), 162
Schneider, Stanley, 161
Schopenhauer, Arthur, 22–23, 41
Schoville, Amelia, 141
Schoville, Rick, 145
Science (magazine), 103
Scopes, John T., 57, 58
Seneca, 35, 45
serotonin, 46
60 Minutes (TV news show), 53, 86
Slepian, Barnett, 101
Smith, Wesley J., 92
Socrates, 42, 45, 65
Sonnier, Patrick, 149
spina bifida, 116, 122, 123
Stanford Law Review (journal), 168
Stoics, 35, 42
Stone, Irving, 162
suffering, 67, 90, 94
  defining excessive, 30
  and palliative care, 75
  seen as senseless, 69, 82, 83
suffocation, 77
suicide, 12
  affects others, 33–36, 45
    due to societal views, 35, 36, 44
  of AIDS patients, 47
  assisted by nonphysicians, 68
  breaks human solidarity, 25, 27–28, 30–31
  causes suicide, 42, 44, 47
  of children, 35–36, 42, 45
  deprives society, 20–21, 33, 36–39, 45–46
    of inspiring models, 39–40
    is an elitist opinion, 37
  due to mental illness, 19, 24, 41, 46, 76, 89
  increases interclass hatred, 46
  is an individual choice, 23, 25, 28, 29–30, 56–58
  is need to feel in control, 90
  is not a competent response, 75–76
  is not an individual choice, 28–29, 31, 48
  is not irrational, 64
  is response to disconnection, 30
  of Native Americans, 47–48
  as noble death, 35, 42
  philosophical arguments against, 20–23
  religious objections to, 19–20, 21, 65, 84
  should not be allowed, 44, 50
    for ill or disabled people, 48–49
  societal response to, 31, 35